D0406002

EDGE SEASONS

OTHER BOOKS BY BETH POWNING

Seeds of Another Summer: Finding the Spirit of Home in Nature
Shadow Child: An Apprenticeship in Love and Loss
The Hatbox Letters

a **MEMOIR**

EDGE SEASONS BETH POWNING

Alfred A. Knopf Canada

PUBLISHED BY ALFRED A. KNOPF CANADA

Copyright © 2005 Powning Designs Limited

Parts of this book were previously published, in slightly different form, in the *New Brunswick Telegraph-Journal*. The chapter "Mingled Deaths" first appeared, in slightly different form, in *Vox Feminarum: The Canadian Journal of Female Spirituality*.

LIBRARY AND ARCHIVES CANADA CATALOGUING IN PUBLICATION

Powning, Beth
Edge seasons / Beth Powning.

Includes bibliographical references.
ISBN 0-676-97641-7

1. Powning, Beth. 2. Authors, Canadian (English)—21st century—Biography. I. Title.

PS8631.086Z463 2005   C813.'6   C2005-901021-5

First Edition

Printed and bound in the United States of America

www.randomhouse.ca

2 4 6 8 9 7 5 3 1

To the valley's next generation:
Jake, Sara, Maeve, and Bridget

To Peter, always

And to the Acadian forest and all its creatures
May you survive

CONTENTS

IN THE BEGINNING

THE NUTSHELL

After we married at the age of nineteen, Peter and I lived in a tiny house known as "The Nutshell." It was the summer of 1969, and we were university students. We had met on a blind date at my campus, just north of New York City. Peter wore wire-rimmed aviator glasses, bell-bottom jeans, and T-shirts with red and blue stripes. He was tall, with shoulder-length brown hair and a gap between his two front teeth. He had blue eyes and a funny last name. I'd just returned from a summer spent at a work camp in the mountains of Mexico. I wore huaraches and sweaters with threadbare elbows. I wanted to be either an actor or a writer. He studied art.

Our parents thought it was unseemly, in those years, to live together unwed, so we were married and moved to the town where I'd grown up—near to the University of Connecticut, for Peter, and a commute to Sarah Lawrence College, in Bronxville, for me. It was a small town, its village centre built along the ridge of a hill, with nineteenth-century houses shaded by giant maples and the surrounding countryside still a patchwork of small dairy farms.

The Nutshell had once been a cobbler's shop but had eventually become an annex to the Chelsea Inn. The inn was half-hidden by overgrown American bamboo; its windows were obscured by ancient, sun-browned paper shades. It was my

3

Aunt Mildred's summer place. After her husband died and her children left home, she let it fall into disrepair. Once a month she drove out from her city house in her Thunderbird, carrying trays of mushrooms in its trunk. "A perfect place for them," she told us in her whispery, enthusiastic voice, "dark and warm." Hair skinned into a bun, lopsided lipstick giving her a loopy smile, she collected the rent and stuffed it into her pocket. I watched her go to the inn's side door, where she stooped, fumbling with the key.

Across the village street were two large houses: one had once been my grandparents' summer place, and the other, my uncle's. I had spent my childhood exploring these houses: their attics were filled with oddments from previous generations—spinning wheels, calf-hide trunks, dresses, hats. Their barns were occupied by dusty wooden tools, sleighs, carriages; and there were flower gardens, orchards, beehives. Next to The Nutshell was a house that had once belonged to my aunt's parents. All these houses were now sold, but the family gatherings of my childhood—Fourth of July, or Labor Day, or apple-harvesting weekends—meant that on either side of the street I could push through screen doors and be offered cold lemonade or cookies. From our porch I could see the Congregational Church, where my parents and my great-grandparents had been married. I could see the library where I had learned to love the smell of books. The post office was five minutes' walk away, as was the town's only general store, with its sagging wooden porch and a bulletin board covered with faded, limp announcements.

Peter and I had two marmalade cats and a dog. In the dank undergrowth behind the little house we cleared space for a chicken pen and kept twelve Rhode Island Red hens. In the summer our two pigs lived at my parents' place at the north end of town, in a pen by their pond. We thumbtacked a map of North America to the plaster wall of our living room and studied it. Place was abstract, a yearning based on notion and desire.

༄

Everything happened for the first time: it was our first kitchen, our first living room, our first bathroom. Peter, revealing himself to be both resourceful and energetic, built a bed on posts, accessible by a ladder. There was a claw-footed tub, its porcelain abraded so that the bather's bottom was scoured. The kitchen was like a boat's galley—sink, gas stove, and refrigerator barely left room to move.

Maples burned in the tawny sun: red-orange, freckly gold. The sweet, wormy smell of soil rose on morning mist. The air was restless, filled with migrating birds and the idle dance of spent leaves. The Vietnam War was present in our lives like an inevitable disease. Young men spent their creativity avoiding or sabotaging the draft—feigning injury or illness, mailing pumpkins to draft boards. The future had no shape. I imagined it the way I saw the valley that spread below us—folds of hills holding no known towns or people or stories. Peter and I wanted to migrate, like the birds. We imagined independence, pictured ourselves living in a place surrounded by space and light, its only sounds those of weather.

The Nutshell filled with dried herbs—tansy, thyme, marjoram—hung in string-tied bunches from nails over the kitchen window. We grew a vegetable garden in my parents' west field.

5

We picked wild Concord grapes from the stone walls. I learned to make jam and bread. We acquired an electric mill and ground our own flour. We went down to a farm in the valley and brought home raw milk in metal cans. Butternut squash lined our porch on frosty October mornings. We bought bushels of apples from roadside stands. I lifted racks of canning jars from their boiling bath, the metallic steam flushing my cheeks, and for the first time I felt the satisfaction of having shelves lined with glass jars: pink applesauce with saucer-shaped air bubbles, purple-black grape jam, dried mint. We sold eggs to our neighbours, made Christmas wreaths and peddled them door to door. Peter helped my father split wood. My mother showed me how to make a purl stitch. Cold air on our faces and frozen earth beneath our boots, the smell of baking bread, frost on windowpanes: these things, like first snow, turned, drifted, and coalesced.

MINT TEA

That first autumn of our marriage we visited with another young couple, Bob and Kathy. They, too, lived in my hometown in a rented house.

"What are you going to do after you graduate?" Peter asked.

"Something like this," Bob said, pointing out the window to the remains of a vegetable garden. "But not here. The slime," he added, nodding towards the village, where the church steeple pierced the treetops, "is just over the hill." He meant the factories, malls, highways, and housing developments that were creeping ever closer, displacing cow pastures and orchards.

We drank mint tea and talked about the Peace River Valley in Alberta, shoring one delicious dream up against another. We imagined going in canoes to a place electricity would never find. We discussed building log cabins, setting traplines, hunting, planting gardens in riverside clearings. I imagined what we would take in our canoes.

"What about my piano?" I said.

Over the winter, we honed our vision, until a plan was made to explore New Brunswick, just beyond Maine. We found a book in the library about the Maritime provinces and pored over its photographs. Bob shared his childhood memories of visiting New Brunswick's forests and river valleys. My maternal grandfather's family had lived in a house called Old Oaks in the border town of St. Stephen. At the turn of the twentieth century they'd come south, to Rhode Island. Now we decided to immigrate at the same border crossing. Once we entered Canada we would leave behind a country in turmoil. Neither Bob nor Peter had been drafted: Bob because of a high lottery number; Peter by dint of creating so many headaches for his draft board that he was given a classification that meant "administratively shelved." Still, it would be a relief to step forward into a nation at peace.

THE VALLEY

On the last day of our exploratory trip to New Brunswick, we crossed a covered bridge and stopped the car. Would we go straight to the coast or turn left? We turned left on a dirt road that wound along the contours of a valley. Hills rose on either side, becoming closer and steeper. We drove through a wooded section and emerged, as if stepping through a doorway, into what seemed to us, then, a hidden valley. Farm fields unfolded up the hillsides like green wings. It was May, and yellow hawkweed nodded in breezes that rippled the short, new grass. An old man stood by a fence, hammer in hand. He was bald, toothless.

"Any places for sale around here?"

He pointed down the road, so we drove on and saw, for the first time, the white church and the one-room schoolhouse at the place where another road wound down from the hills. A few farms perched up on the hillsides, looking down on this tiny centre. We passed a meadow, river laced. There it was, as he'd said: a long lane, a farmhouse, a cluster of barns, a row of maples. Two ancient work horses stood beneath the trees. Swallows circled over the buildings. We drove slowly down the lane. There was a "For Sale" sign on the house.

So we purchased the farm. Our friends bought fifty of its three hundred acres. Over the next two years, we spent our summers in New Brunswick; they built a log cabin and a barn, we built a sauna bath and a pottery studio. One spring, we moved to the valley for good, becoming landed immigrants when we were twenty-two years old.

Ten years passed. Our friends raised three children in the log cabin. By the time they were expecting the fourth, they'd grown tired of hauling babies and children and groceries and supplies over the snowy fields on toboggans, for there was no road to their place in winter. They sold the cabin to summer people and moved to a place not far away where the soil was fertile and the fields faced south. There they started a nursery business.

Peter and I stayed on in the valley. We ran a shop in the nearby town and made our living from the sale of his pottery. Later, we took the pottery to an annual ten-day Christmas sale in Toronto. For years I wrote in the earliest hours of the day and published some short stories; I learned to use a camera and began to make photographs. We kept vegetable gardens, chickens, a horse and pony. Together we ran our pottery business. We raised one child—a son, Jake.

Twenty-four years after we turned left at the covered bridge, Jake was seventeen years old. It was his last year of high school, and soon he'd be gone. Peter and I found ourselves, amazed, standing on a threshold. In one short year we'd be just the two of us again, facing middle age.

FALL

THE SAUNA BATH

Peter and I walk through the pasture. We're going to investigate the sauna bath, long fallen into disrepair. The ground is dry. Goldenrod have become brittle sticks, and their flower heads hold clumps of white fluff. Rather than water, the brook is filled with mint and wild iris. Crickets scurry before our boots.

Behind us, like a flock of sheep, are the buildings of our place: white farmhouse, two grey barns, sheds, the pottery studio. Steel roofs shine in the late afternoon sun. The buildings seem small under the high, autumn sky, dwarfed by the fields that roll up to the forested ridge.

I stop to pick blueberries. It was an extraordinary berry summer—wet July, hot August. The berries are now puckery, no longer juicy. Their sweetness is edged with fermentation, like wine. The air, too, is like wine. It carries the scent of blackberries, apples, and bruised mint. Subtly, it has changed, become languorous, heavy with memory. It pulls my mind towards summer, yet smells of fruition. Insects spin, wings shining in the southerly light, making the most of days that seem like the long blink of heavy eyelids.

೪

SEPTEMBER 5, 1994: *Too many things to do. I don't see what's before my eyes but always think of what I have to do next. Minnie stepped on a nail, so P gave her shots today—three huge needles of penicillin. She reared and thrashed while J and I held onto her halter. Then we soaked her hoof in Epsom salts and hot water. The house full of kids: Jake, Tanya, Jeff, Krista, Amy. I worked in the studio, packed pots till four. After supper, folded laundry—wind-dried sheets, faded T-shirts. J playing the penny-whistle on the porch, then coming in to tell me why he wants to break up with K. Too intense, just wants to be friends with her.*

I have so little time of inner calm, inner peace. I am tormented by self-doubt. I feel the season of the age I am now—forty-five. It's the season of endings, of regrets, of wistfully hanging on, of gathering up. I feel my life falling away behind me. One of the things that comforts me is the thought that my parents, J's grandparents, have made me who I am and that I impart that to my son, so their spark kindles my life, and I pass it on. I dread losing them.

Last night I read a poem by Gary Snyder. It was called "The Bath." Made me remember a forgotten ideal, how P and I used to feel, used to be. Lately, P has been using a fancy leather time-task-organizer. He was sitting at the kitchen table, scribbling in it. I sat across from him and made him listen:

> *Clean, and rinsed, and sweating more, we stretch*
> *Out on the redwood benches hearts all beating*
> *Quiet to the simmer of the stove,*
> *the scent of cedar*
> *And then turn over,*
> *murmuring gossip of the grasses,*
> *talking firewood . . .*

When we were living in The Nutshell, we met a family who had come from Finland. Before they began construction on their house, they built a sauna bath. Inspired, we bought a book called *The Finnish Sauna* and planned a sauna bath during the winters before we moved north, drawing sketch after sketch of a small log building surrounded by pointy trees. We imagined the sauna bath as a ritual that would shape our life—a weekly communion with stars, wind, and icy brook water.

In the first years we lived on the farm, Peter began every Saturday by starting a fire in the sauna. Six or seven times over the course of the day, he went up across the fields to stoke it. By suppertime the temperature topped 200 degrees Fahrenheit, the round beach rocks piled on the firebox were hot, and steam curled from a trash can of water. Meanwhile, I made rye bread and cleaned the house. I changed the bedsheets and made a light meal—fresh bread, carrot soup. After supper we walked up through the darkness carrying backpacks of towels, bathrobes, and a Thermos of tea. When there was snow, we went on skis.

The sauna was on a knoll hidden in the trees. It was a small blockhouse: the top storey, a changing room, was made of weathered boards and overhung the lower storey, the log cabin bath. A kerosene lamp swung from the upper-storey porch. When we arrived, we stuck our skis in the snow. I climbed up a log with notched steps, clinging to a rope, and leaned on the porch railing, watching as Peter scraped embers from the stove and cast them into a pile by the brook. They flared and pulsed in the darkness like a slumbering dragon.

We sat naked in the sauna. We could hear the thin trickle of the brook, and the candlelight made the peeled logs seem soft as our own young skin.

❧

"Remember?" I said to Peter, after I read the Gary Snyder poem out loud.

He glanced up from his organizer, too busy with plans to connect with my thoughts.

"We had more time then," he answered. He was sitting at the kitchen table, poised on the edge of a chair with his knees bent, ready to run.

He runs everywhere in a steady jog. Aside from the production pottery that he's made ever since we moved here, from which most of our income is derived, he creates mixed-media sculptural work that is exhibited in international shows. He wins awards for this work in glass, clay, and bronze, making pieces that push limits. He treads dangerous paths, takes risks, has spectacular failures that precede breathtaking successes. At the same time as he's making pottery, he melts glass or bronze in crucibles. Late at night he'll pour the molten liquid into moulds. There is barely time to breathe, it seems.

In early fall, we begin preparing for the show in Toronto where we sell Peter's raku pottery: bowls and vases, plates and trivets. We've done this for all the years of Jake's childhood, and it's no longer exciting, but necessary. Jake insists this year that because he's seventeen he'll take care of the place when we go. We worry and demur, postponing argument. There's a frequent rampaging of teenagers through the rooms of our high-ceilinged, plaster-walled house. We worry about leaving him the car. Rural kids have to drive everywhere. Jake and his friends reassure us, realizing our anxiety. "We'll be fine," they say, bundling into vans. We try to believe them, waving as they careen dustily down the long driveway.

In spite of our busyness, we make time to take a hike, however brief, every day. This is the year we begin making trails in our woods, calling them by name: "The Ridge Trail," "The Brook Trail," "The Moss Trail." For years we've spent our energies on our immediate surroundings—making gardens, planting trees, stripping wallpaper, building studios, digging a pond, making swings or treehouses—and have gone into the woods infrequently, and then only to follow the sketchy tire tracks of old logging trails. But this year we find ourselves walking away from house and studio, seeking the forest's heart.

In our back hall, where spiderwebs veil the window, there are walking sticks—some peeled, others varnished, some with a twist of burl that serves as a handle. We put on hiking boots, take our sticks, and go to the woods. Our routes are circular, the only destination coming home again, and so the trails evolve. We realize that walking the same path daily is like learning a language: woodchips on the path indicate a woodpecker's hole; purple spruce cones appear, oozing sap; one day there's a new cluster of Indian pipe—transparent stalks bent by strange, colourless flowers. The bookcase by the couch begins to fill with books about ferns, mushrooms, wildflowers, trees.

Windowsills fill with rocks, a duck skull, cow's teeth. In the sherry glasses, there's a robin's egg, a warbler's breast feather. Vases hold dried lily stalks and our mantelpieces become crowded with a witchy jumble: racoon skulls, wasps' nests, bird bones, dragonflies.

So, when I suggest that we resume taking sauna baths, the idea is like the thread of an unseen tapestry in which we're meshed. It has a yearning twist that is familiar. It's as though the idea has not been generated by me but has been waiting to be found, like all the things we bring home from our walks.

❧

Once, the fresh-peeled logs of the bathhouse and the roof's cedar shingles were golden as October leaves. But when we stopped taking sauna baths, wind blew open the door of the upper storey. The changing room filled with snow. Its floor rotted, the wood stove fell into the bath. The notched log pulled down the porch. A window collapsed from its frame.

Today, we step over broken glass, pieces of window-sash, chunks of putty. I push open the door of the sauna. I can still smell the fragrance of resin and smoke, but now it's wreathed with the chill odour of compacted soil and rotting wood. Sunlight shafts into a place never meant to be lit, like a desecrated shrine. There are remains of Jake's childhood use of this place as a fort: a sheepskin given to us as a wedding present, an Oriental carpet, a deer skull, a collection of rusty ten-inch spikes. The place is strewn with feathers from a sodden pillow.

The floorboards have crumbled into a rock-filled pit that once drained the hot, soapy water from our bathing.

"Porcupines," Peter says.

The place is filled with porcupine droppings—heaps of round, sawdusty pellets.

Peter's boots crunch window-glass as he circles the building. "We'll make a good sturdy set of stairs," he says, kicking the notched log. I imagine the calculations he's making, whereas I'm thinking of standing in the snow, wearing nothing but rubber flip-flops. "Maybe I can get Kevin to help." He's speaking of our neighbour. Kevin and his wife, Patricia, have four small boys and live in the notch of the hill. I can hear the school bus shifting gears as it comes down from their house. We decide that we'll phone them and ask if they'd like to make a project with us of renovating the sauna.

The future haunts me. Its diminishing span makes me feel all the things I haven't done yet and may never have a chance to accomplish. Lately, I've stared out our bedroom window at the roof of the decaying sauna bath, just visible through the trees. It makes me feel how swiftly our lives are passing. I'm glad Peter understands my impulse to repair it.

We walk back over the field, our steps brisk. Peter wants a pencil and piece of paper so he can sketch the plans that form in his mind. I feel closer to him, the way I feel when we embark on our walks. I stoop to gather a handful of wrinkled blueberries, sensing a small shift in focus as impulse nudges us towards making a life rather than a living.

WILD GEESE

SEPTEMBER 10, 1994: *Went to see Dr. K about chronic indigestion. He says I'm doing too much, have to cut some things out of my life. I'm on the landfill committee, and I have to photograph a story on hardy kiwis. Recently, we let our bookkeeper go, and I took over the job. I'm also the shipping department. I do the gardens, the house, the cooking. I'm always saying to myself "Everything's under control"—and then something gets out of control. If there's a moment of calm, I feel my mind seeking something to be worried about. I strive but feel that I fail. I feel stretched, without depth. I feel wellings of inexplicable, unfocused fury. Endlessly, I make more work for myself.*

Came home and flew J's kite. As I ran, the string reeled out, the kite soared and plummeted like a live thing. It's hazy, warm, and the trees are beginning to turn. Six sparrow hawks are playing in updrafts over fields. Supper on porch, with a cool wind rising at sunset. P back to studio to crate up that bronze piece that's going to Japan. J off to babysit Patricia and Kevin's boys.

I've begun to write again. I wrote when Jake was a baby, rising at 4:30 and working until he woke. In those years I published some short stories and then wrote a novel that did not find a publisher. Discouraged, I stopped writing other than in my journal, and I channelled my creative energies into child-rearing, gardening, community work, and photography. Several years ago, studying a slide on my light table, words came drifting up like silver bubbles, describing what my camera had captured.

A strand of spiderweb, beaded with dew, bent my heart towards my own expression—something only words could shape. For the next two years I worked on a book inspired by my photographs, until finally it seemed finished.

I haven't dared seek a publisher, and now the manuscript lies on a shelf in my study, a slope-ceilinged room with cracked plaster walls painted white, a wood floor, and two narrow windows facing east. When Jake was about ten, I realized that I'd outgrown my makeshift barnboard desk in the corner of the living room and claimed for my own the spare bedroom over the kitchen. My projects—diaries and writing folders, camera equipment and notebooks—are stacked on pine shelves that cover the south wall. In a bookshelf by the small wooden door are books about spiders, birds, animal tracks, mushrooms, ferns, apples. There's a pine cupboard filled with slide files. My desk snugs into a corner facing a low wall covered with postcards, newspaper clippings, snapshots. There are feathers in mugs, and a white saucer holding bird bones. It's my own room, filled with my own things. I honour the concept with a framed poster of Virginia Woolf that hangs on the east wall.

Both Peter and I, despite our desires to write or make sculpture, work in the pottery full time. He no longer sits at his potter's wheel to throw. There are only so many years one can sit, hunched, twisted. Instead, he devised a method to throw while standing. He attached a metal bar to the ceiling, welding a frame to it that holds a small pillow. He stands like a captain at a wheel, feet separated, back pressed into the pillow, his wheel set on a wooden stand so it's at chest level. He works at his wheel, either throwing new pots or trimming leather-hard pieces, for four or five hours a day. We have one full-time and several part-time employees. We calculate how many orders we need to cover our overhead expenses, and how many more to make a profit. During the day the world drifts past the windows of the barnlike studio, and I glance up from my work—writing invoices, taping cartons—and see solitary birds streaking high over the fields.

By mid-September the birds have begun to congregate. They wheel in dark clouds, heading south. In the woods there's a sense of absence; the rustling leaves are inanimate, unthreaded by the flute of thrush or robin. Along the country roads, telephone wires sag like strands of jet beads, organizing masses of starlings who wait as if for some message they must all receive at once. We hear the gabbling bark of geese, unmelodic as a tuning orchestra, and run out to the studio deck, shading our eyes and seeking the familiar hieroglyphic. The birds are returning from the arctic tundra. They sweep down from the hills, flying so low over the studio roof that we can hear the gabble separate into individual honkings. The lead bird carves the air like a ship's prow, marking the apex of a V; behind, the ragged line shifts, then resolves into its signature. Swiftly, they pass and become a wishbone in the sky, rising, falling, beating their way down the valley towards the blue hills.

After Peter has returned to his potter's wheel, I stand on the deck listening to the whisper of wind, staring at the place where the wishbone became a tiny, wiry scratch. Then I look at the vegetable garden, where blue jays hang upside-down on the sunflower heads, busily pecking. On the bean trellis, scarlet runner-bean pods are dry as ancient linen. It occurs to me that only infants, or Buddhas, can see the world as it truly is. Whatever is happening in my life changes the way things appear to me. Blue jays, runner beans, geese: all drift in a sea of perception, endlessly mutating. This, I think, is how eras are formed. For a while the associations stay constant, and later I remember how the world seemed to be in that time.

I no longer hear the word *Canada* as I once did, when it quivered like the cry of a loon, evoking boundlessness. I can barely remember how, when we first came to this farm, nothing was layered with memory, so I saw with the brazen clarity of a child. That era has long vanished. Many eras have rolled one into another. Here I stand on the studio deck in the autumn of my forty-fifth year and think of the child we raised in this place, a son who is leaving soon to start his own life.

Long after I can no longer see them, I hear the faint echo of the geese's wild barking. Then they are gone, and the shadows seem longer, colder. Another winter is almost upon us. Dispersal is one point on the wheel of life. Birds, wasps, blackberry seeds, baby spiders, maple keys: all spin, wander, and settle. Geese, and sons, fly away.

I slide open the studio door and return to the pile of shipping forms on my desk.

BADMINTON

It's as if he wants to make me hate him so I'll be glad to see him go. No one has ever provoked such blinding red rage in me. *What is this about?* I'm driving the pickup truck to the high school gym where we're going to have a mother–son evening together playing badminton, and he's sitting next to me, pressed against the door, hand on the handle as if, should I slow down, he might wrench the door open and jump out. Even as we're arguing, I've forgotten where this conversation began. He frightens me with his absolute certainty of being right. He notices my slightest wavering or weakness and attacks. He's a superb tactician. Our rising voices are like dissonant music, words lost in sound and rhythm. "You don't understand," he pronounces. "I do." "No, *you don't.*" Like a slap across the face—No, you *don't*. Such bitterness, loneliness, pride. I have become faceless, no longer *me*. I am the shape, sound, taste, and texture of the childhood he needs to trample.

He does wrench open the door when I slow for the turn to the parking lot. I stamp on the brake as he jumps out. He slams the door and strides away, both hands in jean pockets. I park, climb out slowly. I take my racquet from the seat, pause, and then pick up his, too. My doctor is coming down the sidewalk, wearing sneakers and a light jacket, carrying his racquet.

We'll never have another fight like this. I could not bear it.

"Where's Jake?" he says immediately. He sees through my smile. He's had teenagers.

I lift my hand but can't speak. He turns to look, sees my son passing the car dealership, heading towards the train tracks.

We go in to the school together. He holds the door for me. I sense how he's tipped his face, slightly, to gaze into mine, but I can't look at him. Our family isn't simply shifting towards a new shape. We have to be shattered, first—then lie in pieces.

APPLESAUCE

We wake to a white world, grasses swept low by frost. There's a new light in the house, a prismatic shimmer. Everything else—the red leaves of last summer's roses, the shrivelled hawthorne berries—lies utterly still.

Steam rises with the sun, and the autumn morning bakes like apple pie. Jake runs down the long driveway. I lean from the door, waving, and can see across the south pasture to the church and the one-room schoolhouse, now empty. Two bright patches, pink and blue, are the jackets of sisters, Amy and Alyson. I hear their voices as they call to Jake.

I go upstairs into his room and look down at the white frost on the lawn that next year will not be blackened by a boy's footprints. Jake spends so much time with friends that this room is beginning to feel abandoned, like a shell he once inhabited. The thumb-sized Dungeons and Dragons figures are dusty. The tarot cards are untouched. My feet slip on a pile of comic books.

Emptiness surrounds me. Within it, I'm a mother without a child. I'm the bear who can lumber into the forest seeking her own berries. I'm the goose who can fly south, unfettered. I'm any woman whose arms and hands remember the shape of a small body, pressed close. The empty room, like the frozen grasses, retains only the shape of the past.

I see Sue, our full-time employee, driving beneath the row of maples. Her car eases over ruts in the dirt lane as she squints in blue cigarette smoke. Peter has left for the studio. He wears sneakers to abet his running between outbuildings: pottery, woodshop, foundry.

Yesterday he lost an entire kiln load of pottery to glaze failure. He was depressed and irritable. At suppertime, Jake was angry and wouldn't tell us why. We shouted at each other. Doors slammed. An hour later, after a phone call from a friend, he was exuberant, but I remained tense. At bedtime a teacher phoned, concerned about Jake's unfinished assignments. After a day of worry, pacification, rage, I lay sleepless, anxiety coiling in my muscles.

On this September morning, as I gaze out the window, seeing the frost-starred timothy lying in swaths, sudden serenity touches me, breaks the day open, and I redesign my morning. Instead of packing pottery, I'll make a fire in the cookstove and open the kitchen windows. I'll polish furniture, scour the sink, fold sheets, bake muffins. I'll do these things mindlessly, as I might stroke a dog, humming softly.

Downstairs, I fill the teakettle and stand listening to the fire's crackling snap. I'm gazing at a bushel basket of wild apples. They are small, streaked with red like a stormy sunset. Everywhere in this valley, apple trees grow wild. They squat in hedgerows, half hidden by chokecherries. They grow on riverbanks, crowd mailboxes, and strew skirts of apples over hoof-pocked pastures. Smothered by spruce trees, they become twiggy, spiked with dead branches. No matter how crowded or wind stunted, they produce apples: tiny, hard, and bitter or amazingly sweet, and sometimes even juicy.

I decide to make applesauce and lift the basket onto the table. I fall into a rhythm, cupping an apple with one hand and cutting with the other. My wrist pivots; the apple splits with a moist crack. Two swift chops on the scarred wood of the kitchen table, and the apple is quartered. I gather the sections, drop them into a saucepan. They ping against the metal, rattle down. The amber seeds gleam as if freshly varnished. Dried leaves fall from stem-ends, scratch across the floor.

And I notice how, even on this morning of incandescent beauty—sun stroking the speckly orange maples, poplar leaves rippling like wavelets—I'm burdened with imperatives. *You should. You didn't. You should not have. You could have.* I stand watching steam rising from my simmering apples, pale-skinned as they reduce to sauce, and I'm thinking how it's not sunlight that I watch settling in the fiery hearts of nasturtiums, not rain that I see dropping into the pond soft as fish mouths, but time—time, now, that burns in the glowing leaves; time that frightens me.

❧

SEPTEMBER 20, 1994: *My moods go up and down. I have an idea for something I might write but feel too fractured, too pressured. I keep sensing that I've lost some spark, some sense of joy. I'm sick of the constant pressure to produce, maintain, create—make the annual fall studio show, produce new brochures, update the mailing list, find new shops, generate orders. Yet it was a halcyon day, and P and I walked up the Hammond Brook Trail; brushed through beds of pale, hay-scented fern; heard a bird calling and flapping, unseen. Supper at Pete W and Judith's in town. We stood on the flat roof of their café and watched hot-air balloons rise one by one from the ball field. They sailed over the town like matronly ladies, their propane burners making occasional spluttering roars. Tonight I'm sitting by the kitchen stove writing in my journal. J is wearing earphones. He's singing, cowlike, in fractured snatches and perusing a book of tattoos. P is fussing with a*

27

heart monitor he's been given to wear for a week, since he's been having premature ventricular contractions. Dr. K says these PVCs are common and nothing to worry about, but to quell P's anxiety about them he sent P to a specialist, who also is not concerned but wants to get some baseline information. Strange to think that life is half over . . .

DEER ANTLERS

It's a grey afternoon, after rain. I'm climbing up the slope above the waterfall. The first summer we lived on the farm we followed one of the brooks that came twisting down out of the spruce trees at the edge of the pasture and were thrilled to discover, deep in the woods, a secret gully. Its steep, close hills pocketed the sound of falling water as the stream sleeked over moss and then fell, twenty feet, in a shattered spume.

My feet splay sideways; my heart pounds. Behind me, the waterfall breaks on boulders. The sound diminishes as I push up the hill, circling back towards home.

I stand for a minute, panting, listening to the intermittent drip of water, hoping to hear a distant, drifting coyote call or an owl's hoot. But the woods are quiet. I take a step and there, at my feet, is a deer antler. I pick it up. It fits the curve of my arm like a lyre. The knob where it broke from the deer's skull is brown and nubbly; the antler is worn to a grey patina where it bends and branches. It's rare to find them, even though the males lose their antlers every winter after the fall breeding season and begin to grow a new set every spring. This antler must have dropped off last year and spent a winter lying under the snow. I wonder if the deer felt lopsided until the other one fell off. By now he'll have a brand new set. He'll have rubbed off the velvety skin and be raring to fight for a female.

I stand in the gathering dusk, holding the antler.

Something of me will disappear when there is no longer a child in the house, a person who once fit inside my body as this bone fits my arm. The thing that will disappear is like a gift I had no idea I was giving. "Thank you," my son will say, gathering it up and turning away.

Along the ridge trail, beds of reindeer moss spread like mist beneath the spruce trees; the dark spruces are jewelled with unlit water drops that tremble from the tip of every needle. Ferns are bent, their stalks pulpy. There's not a breath of wind.

As I walk, I'm thinking of my unpublished book lying on its shelf. It's like a song I once heard and put to paper. No one else hears it, as they would if they were to read my words. I listen and can hardly hear it myself.

"Never to allow gradually the traffic to smother / With noise and fog the flowering of the spirit," wrote the poet Stephen Spender.

I come out into the sodden field and swing down the hill, cradling the antler in the crook of my arm. The house is empty— Peter and Jake are in town. I carry the antler to my study and set it on a shelf next to a pile of beach stones and a sepia-toned photograph of an unknown relative wearing a Civil War uniform. The antler has no more connection with the soft-nosed deer who grew it than do gravestones with the people whose names they bear. Yet it connects me to my moment of finding: curved bone gleaming against wet leaves, haunting as sourceless music.

❧

SEPTEMBER 28, 1994: *I've been in a hiatus—a deep pause. I live from day to day, telling myself that it's okay just to go on, make meals, do rote work. But I miss . . . myself. The layer of dreaming, poetry. Someone seems gone, like an old friend. What is the motivation to create? Desire, love, simple delight, not fear or the need for recognition. I talked about this with P. We both need, he said, to remember that we have time. There should not be such pressure to produce huge quantities of . . . anything. But neither one of us feels we have time. Who I am, I told him, seems to change as I go from room to room of the house. One minute I'm a gardener, the next a mother, the next a potter's assistant. You're all of those things, he said, and that makes you who you are. But I feel that I'm sleepwalking through my days.*

MINGLED DEATHS

My parents come to visit. They still live in the house of my childhood. It's an old red farmhouse in Connecticut, surrounded by fields and overhung by the swaying branches of a weeping willow. When I talk to them on the phone, as I have on Sunday mornings for decades, I imagine their house so vividly that I might actually be there as I talk. I hear the creak of floorboards in the upstairs hall as my mother walks from her bedroom; see the dried geranium leaves on the blue windowsills; smell the faint whiff of leftover smoke coming from the fireplace; and hear how my father makes the back-door latch clatter, coming in from his woodshop.

They arrive, tired after the ten-hour drive. Although their house is always exactly as I remember it when I visit, they look smaller when they come here and I feel younger, my voice rising in tone as I embrace them, adjusting to being a daughter once again, their little girl. They, too, seem startled by me, as if I am older or sadder. Then they see Jake, who comes out the back door, and all of us settle into the places we've grown used to—familiar niches. Our son makes them less parents, more grandparents, and, as Jake grows older, we treat my parents with increasing tenderness, like the precious beings we realize they are becoming.

They visit for a week. One day my father watches a hawk from the studio window. I see how the skin of his eyelids is delicate, almost translucent. My mother, I notice, has grown stoop-shouldered, although she is still light-footed in her sneakers. When they leave, Peter and I stand in the driveway, waving. I smile until the car turns at the mailbox. Then my face breaks. He puts his arms around me. We stand in the mist-shrouded morning. There's no sound but the plaint of a jay. The grasses are bent by water drops. *All of us, getting older.*

It's Saturday, and I spend the morning in the attic, finding books for the library book sale. My rummaging makes a racket, like a rat scrabbling in a barrel. I lift cardboard boxes, half-filled with detritus from one of Jake's room-cleaning attempts. There are piles of old coats, music books, camping equipment. Pottery experiments: a raven perched on a salt-glazed toilet; a doughnut-shaped wine decanter. Stacks of silk-screen frames from the mid-seventies, when Peter applied photographic images to porcelain pots. A blue toy chest, like a cedar sarcophagus layered with stuffed animals.

I page through a spiral-bound notebook filled with Jake's drawings. I lift a skirt that I wore in the mountains of Mexico when I was eighteen. I hold the toilet-perched raven in my hand. I think of all the people I have known, pressed in their epochs like dried flowers. I cling to the past, write of it, dream of it. I haven't been able to accept that it is gone. I long to have it back again. I feel I didn't appreciate any of it enough. The past aches in my throat, and I don't realize that what I'm mourning is myself.

I sit in the attic and listen to the first soft tip-taps of rain on the steel roof.

❧

Rain breaks from a low mist that has ghosted over the hills for days, veiling all but the dark spires of spruce and fir. The trees gloom and then disappear, like boats in fog.

After lunch Peter and I cross the lower meadow and follow the brook into the woods. In summer this same path wound through ferns: ostrich, cinnamon, interrupted, woodsia, hayscented. By mid-summer the ferns were waist-high, and the trunks of beech and maple rose from a feathery green sea. Leaves and ferns sighed and rustled, lissome in the summer breeze. Now there's only a soft, yellow-brown tangle of collapsed fronds, pinnae furled or missing, stalks bent double.

The rain intensifies. Motionless leaves begin to nod; the splatting patter augments, like a new melody, the steady running of the river.

We're looking for mushrooms. The wet forest exhales, yields its sweet decay, and I can smell the fibre of stumps, the earthy sharpness of leaves. Rain slides down stems, gleams like oil, pocks the river's pools.

We find constellations of tiny, string-stemmed white mushrooms; orange slime moulds rubbery in the clefts of trees; poisonous amanitas on sturdy stems. Everywhere there are mushrooms: chanterelles, penis-like stink horns, red russulas, dead-man's fingers, scarlet waxy caps. Beneath a fallen spruce tree are clumps of coral fungi. Wolf's-milk slime grows on a dead log, oozing pink paste. In a clearing, three destroying angels spread translucent gills over bunchberries, whose red, blade-shaped leaves bend towards their burden of one quivering raindrop.

The mushrooms thrust their fleshy caps through anthills, reindeer moss, or the needle-strewn soil of thickets. Like humans, they have no means of extracting life from sunlight; buzzard-like, they are eaters of the dead. They're the last fruiting bodies of summer, and their mycelia probe decaying trees, leaves, and twigs, producing cell-destroying enzymes, releasing nutrients, making soil. Without preamble they erupt, red-orange or ivory, dew-beaded, flecked with the papery remnants of veils. The ancient Greeks believed they burst from Zeus' lightning.

"Look, over there!"

We kneel. It's a dense cluster of reddish-brown mushrooms growing from decaying leaves. Flat caps ride slender stalks. We look them up in the book Peter brought in his day pack. He lingers longer than I do, turning pages. "Could be a tufted coin-cap," he says. I stand, brush my knees, walk on.

Their presence means that another summer has stabbed past. My footsteps are quiet on the path, softened by wet leaves. I tally up the summer's visitors.

"Peter," I say, stopping. "Do you realize we had forty days of back-to-back company?"

He's stuffing the book into the pack, pulling the drawstring.

"Sometimes," he says, falling in stride behind me, "I'd wake up and forget who was in the guest room." Cousins, parents, friends, friends of friends—the house fell into chaos.

We walk slowly through the warm rain. I'm pondering summer: how it used to be my favourite season. Once, summer blossomed with present moments, like a bush heavy with lilacs: sweet air fingered the corners of rooms, screen doors slammed, paper lampshades swung in winds that swept through the house. But last summer I felt stampeded by time—or by its lack. I regretted the passing of the delphiniums, whose tender blue blossoms I did not appreciate; I did not stop to pick wild strawberries or watch, on a day of wind, how the timothy grass passed shadows up the hills.

One day, I remember, Patricia and Kevin's older boys came with unlaced sneakers asking to swim in the pond. I stood in the back door watching them going through the fields, the towels on their shoulders becoming bright spots as they dwindled. Field and sky soared over the children; they became small as insects, specks of colour in the stirring, blowing, growing world. Leaning against the door frame, I thought—*I have no time.*

Was it the children who were living in time, and I who was living without it? Or was it the other way around?

In August, the sky was black and I could smell rain. I went into the vegetable garden and closed the gate. A fence separated me from the wildflowers and the blowing grasses. Thunder crumpled, far off, like the hills grumbling. The garden tossed under a dark sky, in a warm wind, and I realized that it was at its peak of loveliness, perfect as the baby swallows teetering on the phone lines. But the short northern summer rolled onward, violent in its condensed trajectory, and I felt the pressure of the turning planet, the shortening days. I felt as though I barely had time to complete the harvest. Days later, the dillweed began to turn to seed, beet greens turned brown at the edges. I lugged feed bags filled with potatoes into the earthy darkness of the root cellar, slashed woody broccoli stems, twisted ears of corn from stalks—just in time to save everything before the killing frost. Then the sweet peas hung like crumpled bags. Nasturtium vines sprawled, soft and white as cooked spaghetti. Thatch-coloured corn leaves turned on the slightest breeze, rattling. I leaned on the garden fence, thinking: *another summer has gone fleeting past while I knelt in the soil, creating my beautiful garden, knowing how it would be stilled.* I wrote in my journal: "Nothing stays. I feel my life sliding behind me, all its images—sun on wallpaper, Easter Sunday, wedding vows, my baby son—like so many flower petals, strewn on water."

In the quiet woods no birdsong creases the irregular dripping; nothing, save the mushrooms, is beginning. And I feel as though I'm walking in summer's after-light, in the washed stillness of an ebbing storm.

Peter stands by the brook, hood pulled forward. He stirs the water with his walking stick. On a mud bank in midstream, the summer's grasses have collapsed. He points out the place where they wave and sweep in the current.

Amid the remains of summer, I don't feel the unfolding calyx of life but see only endings. I listen to the forest's profound calm. I want to induce such stillness within myself. I want to absorb, like the mushrooms, the lack of regret, the deep mulch of mingled deaths.

CLEANING UP THE SAUNA BATH

It's October 7th, a warm, misty Saturday. Poplar leaves are limp as worn dishcloths. Golden, freckled, they curl, funnelling water droplets. The air smells of stems and wet twigs. The brook is full again and twists through the pasture.

The air is rent by the scraping groan of pried nails. Peter, our neighbour Kevin, and Jake are wielding pry bars, tearing down the rotting second-storey deck of the sauna bath. Peter instructs Jake with a patience that sounds tried: "Take a hammer, Jake. Hammer the pry bar into the board around the nail. The wood's like butter. Watch."

Patricia and Kevin are fifteen years younger than we are and were children growing up in Saskatchewan during the summer we originally built this sauna bath. She's tall and strong, with glossy black hair.

"You're such a good mother, Pat," I remark, raising my voice so she can hear me.

I'm inside the sauna bath. Its roof, or ceiling, is half gone, but it still smells of smoke-saturated spruce logs. I'm squatting in the rock-filled pit, wearing overalls and work gloves, scooping up porcupine droppings with my hands. They are dry, odourless, the size of olives. I dump them into a cardboard box. She's just outside, stooping, picking broken windowpanes from the grass, throwing the shards into a metal bucket.

She laughs, incredulous, and stands with her hand pressing the small of her back. "You should hear me at bedtime."

"No, but you are so patient! And you actually follow through on threats. Remember the time you told the boys they'd have to walk home if they weren't ready?"

"Well. If you have four boys . . ."

She steps into the doorway, black against the light. "Having fun?"

"Time for a coffee break." I scramble to stand splay-legged on the tippy rocks that we brought from a cairn in the nearby woods. Whoever picked these rocks, clearing a field on a cool spring morning, could not have imagined that, one day, they would provide drainage for a sauna bath.

On its little hill, nested within spruce trees, the sauna bath overlooks a marshy meadow, blue with flag iris in June, succeeded by beds of ostrich ferns and buttercups, and spiked in fall with asters, goldenrod, and pink steeplebush. A stream meanders into the meadow and breaks into two: one stream comes to the foot of the little hill; the other flows into a small, deep pool. The tractor is parked under a maple tree, a wagon hitched to its tongue; the boys straggle down to it from the sauna bath, lugging junk for the dump: rotten boards, chunks of mortar, crumbling fire bricks.

Patricia and I dig in our backpacks. Her sons come nosing, like puppies. The youngest is four; the oldest is ten. They exhibit pack behaviour, angling for food. Patricia takes out a bag of cookies, distributes oranges.

"Put the peels in the firepit," she says. She's calm, judicious. The boys walk away, stooping forward, spitting seeds. There's a ring of rocks near the brook where, later, in the cold days, we'll have bonfires.

We sit on the wagon, our feet swinging, watching the men and Jake. We unscrew our Thermoses, pour coffee into the caps.

Only the yellow poplar leaves are left. The maples stand naked; mists blend with their grey bark. Shreds of cloud hang on the hillsides, then disperse, although there is no wind. Our sounds—men laughing, the ring of hammers, the splinter and crack of boards being wrenched, boys' shouts—seem loud, exaggerated, falling against the ripe stillness of a completed season.

We hear the gobble-cry of two ravens and the swish of their wings as they fly low, curious.

"Funny," I say, "how when you've done something like paint a room or reshingle a roof, you think of it as *new* for so long."

"Like kids," Patricia says. "Suddenly they're not babies, then they're not even toddlers."

How insidiously it happens; like the ferns, collapsing. Even when we didn't use the sauna bath, it seemed a component of our lives and informed our self-image. Gradually, its spirit eroded. I no longer made rye bread. Our ritual fell fallow and died. Something left our lives that we had not intended to let go.

It is good that Kevin and Patricia never knew the sauna in its prime. Its genesis is only a story. They can't feel our sense of disbelief at the sight of smashed window sash, ruined flooring, rotten shingles. We lean on their energy. They are delighted with this project, as if it is something new that is being built rather than an abandoned dream resurrected.

I slide off the wagon, pulling on leather gloves. Patricia slides off as well, striding towards the firepit to moderate a spirited argument. I duck back into the sauna, looking up to see that no board is going to fall on me. I actually enjoy what I am doing. The job is simple: pick up rocks, throw them out the door, see porcupine shit rolling into the gap, scoop the droppings with both hands, dump them into a box.

Above me, the men tear down what no longer functions while, one handful at a time, I clean the pit, imagining how, one day, the hot, soapy water will once again trickle past these rocks.

HEARTWOOD

OCTOBER 8, 1994: *Today was a blue-sky day with a watery wind. I stood beneath the maples holding a chunk of heartwood that I picked up from the grass. Heartwood is the colour of bone and so dry that it weighs almost nothing.*

ಎ

For over twenty-five years I've looked out the south windows of our house and seen the maples. I imagine them as saplings, brought down from the woods in a wagon; it's the spring of 1894, and the little trees are wrapped in cloth. Their branches quiver as the wheels tilt over the road's muddy ruts; there's a clop of horse hooves and the watery din of red-winged blackbirds. Someone must have laid a long rope on the ground, counted footsteps between each one, and dug deep holes, setting the young trees in a perfectly straight line between the lawn and the driveway. Perhaps a woman urged her husband to this task. The trees are comforting, like walls or window frames. They stand stalwart in a place of endless change. The farm is surrounded by brooks, crescent-shaped fields, marshy pastures, and copses like wind-swept islands, their margins scraggly with rock cairns. In all this meandering pattern, the sugar maples stand like sentinels, stating a distinction, marking a boundary. Someone longed for order.

Just in the cleft where the branches begin are massive growths of northern tooth mushrooms. Their structure is like a stack of fifteen or twenty toasty-yellow pancakes, smallest ones on the bottom, largest ones on top. The mushroom thrives in the wounds of living sugar maples and rots the heartwood; the tree dies slowly, consumed from within.

I've invested these trees with myself, given them space on my interior shelves. Christmas morning is laced with their ice-glittering branches. Late in March, when days are sunny and nights are cold, we bore into them with a hand drill: moist cambium spirals out, sap wells in the spile and drops into the metal bucket, making the first plinking note of spring. In summer I knead bread in the rustling space of their leaf-sigh. They're wind indicators, bird gatherers. Mourning doves bead their silhouette at winter's sunrise. Migratory flocks return to their shelter, just as I awaken to them, every morning, or listen, in darkness, for their presence. They belong to their space. In October I watch for Orion angling through the treetops with his red-starred shoulder. Their branches snag the crescent moon. A neighbour coming to visit, holding a child's hand, is not unprotected in the cold air as she passes beneath their heavy limbs.

Ever since we discovered that the northern tooth mushrooms are killers, we've attacked the growth, scraped it away, worked fertilizer into the soil at the trees' roots. Still, after every windstorm, the ground is littered with chunks of deadwood torn from the living trees. The wood lies in the grass like the bedsprings and bucket handles that spill from abandoned houses on the back roads.

They're changing. Space is changing.

❧

OCTOBER 8, 1994: *I stood looking up into the maples. Their leaves drop sooner than those of healthy trees. Their crowns are paled by dead limbs. I tried to imagine the day that Peter attacks these trees with a chainsaw, how I will watch their limbs thud to the ground and become reduced to chunks of firewood. I'll console myself by stacking them. Then there'll be an emptiness in the sky; the house will be wind-prey, forlorn, unprotected. I wonder where Jake will be—living somewhere far away, probably: the Outer Hebrides or the Shetland Isles. A barkeep; a Scottish wife and two round-faced sons. We'll fly over to visit, once or twice a year. And here, there'll be fewer cows in the pastures, or none. The old people will have died, and we'll be left—the elders of the community.*

I think that it's sensible to prepare myself. Truthfully, though, I can't imagine the loss of these trees. I'll be heartbroken when they finally go.

Next weekend is Thanksgiving. I was picking dried grasses to soften a bouquet of dead lily stalks and baby's breath, browsing in the fields like a pecking hen, preparing to celebrate another season's passing.

ANIMAL TRACKS

We're surrounded by wild creatures. Everywhere we see evidence of their lives: dead trees are riddled by the beaks of woodpeckers; beetle trails are chewed in rotting bark; under the rim of river-banks, muskrats make holes, round and black as gun muzzles. We find the scat of deer, fox, moose, rabbit, coyote, quail. On warm nights the flute-call of a thrush floats from the woods, while just below our bedroom window racoons squabble, snarling and growling. At dusk we hear the guttural *hoo-hoo* of great-horned owls and glimpse their catlike ears as they perch on fence posts, where they pick at their nocturnal snacks; we find mouse bones on the posts and, once, the bones of Gussie Fink-Nottle, a missing kitten. In the pond, small trout fling themselves so far out of the water that their bodies slap down, sideways, and send water droplets skittering like pearls.

In summer the animals have immunity from our scrutiny. Scat dissolves in rain; paws leave few traces. Now the cloak dis-integrates. Scarcity nudges. As autumn ripens towards its own transformation, it's easier to see animal tracks. Paths hidden by low-hanging alders become obvious; skeletal leaves reveal the press of hoof. The brooks are no longer obscured by beds of fern, and in their muddy verges are squirrel tracks like Japanese brush paintings or the bird-bone prints of racoon paws.

Late one afternoon, after I've taped up the last carton of pottery, I go for a walk. My feet follow the familiar hummocks of one of our trails, but then I decide to break off the path. I pause for a minute, mentally collecting landmarks. *The waterfall. The place we cut the big maple. The steep hillside. Okay.* It's hard to get lost up on the hills, since downhill always leads to a brook or river that funnels into our valley, but possible once you pass deeper into the woods, where the land sweeps into other valleys. I follow the half-moon holes of deer tracks, chopped through rotting leaves. The tracks cross a maze of other trails. I pause, seduced by lures and clues: a distant bird call, the clapping thunder of partridge wings. My eyes seek squirrel middens, feathers, skulls. I kneel to pick at coyote scat with a stick; it's filled with bones, chopped fine. I trace my eyelid with a raven feather.

My jacket rustles and twigs crack under my hiking boots; vacancy precedes me. Summer has broken over this forest like a cresting wave, towering, light-shafted. Now it retreats. I expect revelation or explication. The harsh, poignant cry of a blue jay comes like a mockery.

I scuff up the path next to the brook and lean against a yellow birch we call Big Mama. At her feet is a pool created by a fallen log. Black water bends, breaks into a waterfall; rocks are magnified behind the shifting sheet. In the pool, a froth of bubbles rides an upstream current; farther downstream, a necklace of air spirals up through the water. Beads break the surface and glint, briefly iridescent before they shatter.

My mind falls blessedly quiet. I am touched by a revelation that brushes my mind like a snowflake. *The woods simply exist. Journey and destination are one and the same.*

❧

OCTOBER 20, 1994: *Heavy frost. This morning I went out to the back door and stood smelling the clean, sharp air. I heard odd pinging noises, like cooling metal, and looked over to see the crab apple tree filled with goldfinches, each poised over a clump of tiny apples and attempting to eat them, often frustrated by the apples dropping, with a ping, to the steel roof below. The yellow birds shone in the rising sun.*

Thinking of writing. Wanting to write. The urge is a feeling in my hands, like holding a small globe—something round and complete.

This morning I found this quote from George Eliot's Middlemarch: *"If we had keen vision and feeling of all ordinary human life, it would be like hearing the grass grow and the squirrel's heart beat, and we should die of that roar which lies on the other side of silence."*

I think I understand that: the human roar. But it's nature's silence that fascinates me.

❧

I'm upstairs in my study, snatching a moment at my desk. I write in my journal, enjoying the cut of nib on unlined paper. Peter is in the cellar—I hear a thud and clatter as he throws wood in the furnace. The door has just slammed behind Jake, who, at breakfast, was copying hands from a book of Leonardo da Vinci's drawings. His blonde hair was caught in a ponytail; rimless glasses sat cockeyed on his nose. I glimpsed his older self in his absorbed concentration that was without self-consciousness, tinged with a sadness that he's had since childhood. His artist's scrapbook is filled with pages of hands. The hands he chooses to copy are knotted with age. He tells me that he likes to imagine himself as an old man. I had to pat his shoulder. "The bus, Jake! Get going." This morning he told us that he's decided to apply to the Nova Scotia College of Art and Design. He seems happy about it. This decision sets him apart from us, makes us observe him with respect. Sometimes—often, in fact—there are intimations of an easier relationship to come.

Now I go downstairs, pass through the sunny kitchen. In the boot hall, I put on fleece vest, denim jacket, wool gloves. Lately, I've been taking a brisk circular walk before going to the pottery studio. I step out the back door, walk past the raspberry patch. The leaves are dark purple-red, crusty with frost. I put a leaf in my mouth, looking up at the pearly morning sky, thinking, as the frost melts on my tongue, of how the Bushmen of the Kalahari Desert know the sources of water and remembering how, last night, the sky was dusted with stars—like powder, as if they'd been thrown up in fistfuls.

Thanksgiving is just past. As I walk uphill over the mown field, I realize that the crickets, like the swallows, have vanished without my marking the moment of their disappearance.

I leave behind the half-wild meadows at the top of the hill and push my way into the spruce trees. A smell rises—resin, moss, dead ferns. A long-fallen tree is shingled with turkey tail mushrooms; I squat, riffling them with my thumb. They're leathery and blunt, like a deck of well-worn cards. Now our farm lies far below; through the trees I can see the glint of its roofs. The faint wind-snatched barking of a dog belongs to someone else's world. My preoccupations begin to separate, like bubbles gleaming on sand. Calmness seeps into me, as if I'd stepped into a home whose belongings have found natural resting places. Here, the hay-scented fern is always in the clearing, just beyond the old fenceline. Here, red and orange amanitas always thrust through moss beds. Here's the place where the path is carpeted with red leaves.

Here, too, is the bear's trail. We saw his paw prints last March, in snow, running east–west, going downhill into the dark firs. We knew that these slipper-like pressings were the prints of a bear, even before we saw the five round claw holes.

I stop by a beech whose bark, last time I passed here, was smooth. Now, a bear's claws have shredded it in five places, seeking insects or marking territory. I can see the yellow flesh of inner bark, bits of wood scattered on the trail. I step close, sniff, run a fingertip across the abrasions. In this mute message—a few scratches, a few chips—the forest's vitality reveals itself. On this seemingly changeless and always empty path, a black bear lumbered, nose swaying from side to side, eyes peering. He stopped, just here, and reared to his feet. The scratching of his claws travelled to the ears of other creatures.

Light flickers as a breeze lifts the branches. A leaf wavers and circles on the air like half-burned paper.

I sense presence but hear and see nothing. I see only the remains of a passage.

I plunge down a steep hillside through fir trees that grow so thickly, the air is perceptibly colder. They open into a birch grove where the ground is carpeted with bunchberry. In spring, the ground is white with flowers; in summer, stippled with red berries. Now the bunchberry leaves are translucent and fade into this sere landscape of white bark, lichen, rotting wood. I begin to feel the pressure of the day's work but decide to go to the hollow where the jack-in-the-pulpits grow.

Abruptly, I halt. Next to the path is a hawk's wing. Flies teem on the flesh where the wing was torn from the bird's body. Further along the trail are clumps of feathers still attached to one another, scattered like small, perfect fans. There's the other wing—and a few bones, still bloody.

Kneeling, I pick up the wing and separate one feather from the clinging flesh. Its spine curves, pure as the line of light between sea and sky. The individual barbs cling to one another, bending inward with a mottled pattern. How does a hawk die? I can imagine no predator—and ponder a bird's old age.

At the edge of the east field is a marshy piece of ground, too wet to mow. A pair of marsh hawks cruise up and down our valley, and this marsh is the female's favourite hunting ground. She hovers, wings quivering as she makes subtle shifts over the ferns and wildflowers. She hunts in other places, too; I see her flying along the river in morning mists, cruising over pastures, rising on updrafts. She dives, then lifts from the grasses with talons clutching some small rodent. Her silver-grey mate is elusive; we seldom see him, and then only at the edge of the forest. She, however, in her warm brown feathers, her endless questing, becomes familiar to me, a thread of summer, wild as the cold spice of balsam. I sense her spirit as I watch from the kitchen window and observe the taut set of her shoulders. There is no communion between me and the bird; she has no need of me. Although she must hunt in the open skies, her mystery is undiminished; my heart lifts and quiets whenever I look up, through window glass or screen door, and see her fierce solitude.

In each feather of this bloody wing, her grace lingers.

The yellowy-brown ferns are crumbly, dry, embracing the sun, disintegrating. There's no sense of urgency. All things have run their course: risen, danced, and faded. The power that leapt from the spring soil expires in the amber light—like a bear turning slowly in its cave; like a hawk, falling from the sky.

I sit in the sun, listening to the rush of river water. I should be at work. There are shelves full of pottery to pack. I'll label the boxes so that, when we arrive at the show, we can stack them in the storeroom and know what's inside. Cartons of invitations have arrived from the printer. Labels need to be printed out, envelopes stuffed. We're running out of excelsior and bubble wrap. I close my eyes and picture the cement floor of my packing room, painted salmon-pink and littered with shredded paper. I imagine the sound of the potter's wheel, voices coming from the radio, the fly-specked windows—the day passing beyond the glass.

OCTOBER 21, 1994: *Robert Frost: "A complete poem is one where an emotion has found its thought, and the thought has found the words."*

48

Shall I send my manuscript out into the world? My room is flooded with fall sunshine. The wood-fire furnace rumbles in the cellar. I am reading essays by Maya Angelou. She says a woman must, above all, laugh. Gazing up through my skylight, I see blue sky and a corner of metal roofing. I decided to begin a new book, called Harvest. *I feel an enormous pressure to create something of my own, to find my voice and make it heard. I feel that there's less and less time left in my life for me to do that. I feel like a fragment of what was once whole, a feather torn from a wing. Maybe this is why I collect bones, shells, dried seed casings: they remind me of myself. I long for a peaceful heart and dread another winter, filigreed with Jake's departure.*

I'm living what I once thought of as "my future." I've arrived in this space of time that once was formless and now has a shape: a farmhouse, a northern sky, a son, a husband. Peter and I have been building this life the way wasps build nests, layer on layer, with intense need and single-minded concentration. Now I see that what I once imagined as an attainable place—adulthood—has no substance. It's like frost: vanishes when touched.

The days dawn, ripen, and pass. Bedtime comes around, over and over. "Here we are again," Peter says as we make adjustments to pillows and blankets, seeking comfort. Peter and I turn off our bedside lights, roll over onto our sides, backs pressed together. In the next room Jake stirs a box of pens, Lego, broken cameras. Maybe he's picking through the treasures of his childhood, deciding what to take, what to leave behind.

I think about how I, too, need to move on, remake myself. If my body were a house, I'd get rid of all the things no longer used or needed. I'd furnish myself only with things that work well. I'd be clean, spare, filled with light. I'd be square, sturdy, thick-timbered, with shining floors. I'd tell people to leave me alone, long enough for me to get settled. I'd look out of my own windows and see deep valleys filled with golden-leaved beech trees.

❧

In late October, shadows are lengthening as I begin making supper. Jake's taken the car to school and hasn't yet returned, although the bus has long since dropped off the other valley kids. I make potato scallop, with mushrooms, garlic, and blue cheese, and slide it into the oven of the wood stove. The teakettle spurts steam. I transcribe bits of poetry into my leather-bound journal, which snaps shut with a button made of an Indian-head nickel.

> *. . . frost, starlight.*
> *the creak of boots.*
> *rabbit tracks, deer tracks.*
> *what do we know.*

Gary Snyder, "Pine Tree Tops"

Peter is still in the studio, although our employees—three, at this time of year—have gone home. Until recently we've perceived our lack of leisure as a virtue. Having "no time" was a point of pride. We would bring cartons of raku pottery into the kitchen and sit cross-legged on the floor until late at night scouring soot from the glaze. Now we hire other people to do it. Our expenses rise. Success narrows us.

I snatch moments like forbidden sweets. I sit in my grandfather's rocking chair, between the wood stove and the small-paned window. I rock, eyes closed, as I try to forget my interior list. It's a compendium of adult duties, all the components of running a life: insurance, cheques, food, car, clothes, gifts, bills, social obligations. Peter suggests that I give up some of the things I do. I'm offended and incredulous.

Everything's under control. No one else can do these things as competently as I can.

Sun casts a path across the pine floor. Hanging against the wall are braided onions and dried tarragon. "Frost, starlight . . ." I whisper, and feel a rich, dark loveliness as I say these words. I snap shut my journal and set it on the counter. I put another log on the fire, readjust the dampers, scribble a note, and leave it on a chair in the middle of the room: "Hi, J and P—I've gone to the pond. Back soon. Please check scallop."

I walk down the farm lane past the marsh. Night air rises from wet roots. Red clouds sail in a peach sky, and the fields gleam like copper pans on a firelit wall. I come to the rise and see the pond, surrounded with sand-pale grasses, reeds, husks of turtle-head flowers. I freeze in mid-step.

A great blue heron perches at the end of the dock. One leg is raised, claw clenched. Yellow feathers brush softly around his fierce eye. He stares intently at the water, where his reflection seems only slightly less solid than he is himself.

I lower my foot.

He's almost as tall as I am. His feather-plumed head tucks back into his body, his neck a soft curve between massive blue-grey shoulders. I can see him as clearly as I see Peter across the breakfast table. One white feather is slightly ruffled, out of place, its spine gleaming; the knobby joints of one claw spread against the warm wood, while the other is tucked into his plumage, its claws curling, uncurling. His yellow beak is sharp as scissors. Low light burns in his feathers. I sense his pleasure in the warm rays.

He must be aware of me, yet he doesn't stir a wing or cock his head. I step forward, once, twice. I take five or six stealthy steps, holding my breath.

He stretches his neck. I see his true size as the heavy wings hunch upward, and then the bird is no longer part of the wood, the water, the reeds, but is instantly an element of air, two powerful beats of the great wings veering him up sideways, away from the pond, legs dangling. He croaks once, a call as if to another heron, not to me. His wings rise and fall, and he turns his head southwards. He becomes a black silhouette against the flaming sky, flying low along the alders into the night.

I turn, shading my eyes, thrilled. I watch the heron until he is a speck over the hill, until he vanishes beyond the frieze of trees.

The light has deepened; a breeze touches the reeds. The water breaks into a corduroy of ruby-edged ripples. There is no trace of the heron's presence.

I cross the field and go up to the sauna bath.

Everything rotten or broken or half-attached has been removed. The deck is gone, as is the notched log. Every bit of the window frame has been removed, and the opening is covered with heavy plastic. The upper storey is raised a few inches by stout timbers set on jacks; milled spruce beams have been slid beneath. There's a pile of lumber, bright yellow, for framing a new upstairs floor, for the sauna bath's new ceiling, for a new slatted bath floor and new benches. The grass has been picked clean. I open the door and peek in. The pit is now filled with clean rocks. I look up. I can see far up, through new timbers, to the changing-room's peaked roof.

I take a deep breath of the resin-tinged air. *Sauna smell.* It's been here all along, that lovely smell. Just as, evening after evening, a great blue heron may have been enjoying our dock and we never noticed.

OCTOBER 30, 1994: *One more day and all the fall orders will be packed. Shipped fourteen cartons last week, about eleven this week. J home at four. Great talk with him at supper. He told us that he had a wonderful childhood. Mark C came down from his house on the hill to have P cut his hair. Mark turned fifty-seven this month; bald head with freckles and fringe of grey hair. P set him up in a straight-backed chair and put a towel around his shoulders. Much laughter. Mark told P not to touch his beard: he's going prospecting and needs the warmth. P has an artist's touch with the scissors—snipping, fluffing the ends, snipping again. After Mark left, P had to go back out to the studio to trim pots. It's as relentless as milking cows . . . once the pots begin to dry, he has no choice but to deal with them. I organized a potluck supper club tonight. Once a month we'll meet at one another's houses, up and down the valley. Everyone seems pleased. I feel, lately, as if I have a new job: myself.*

53

Putting myself together; or keeping myself from falling apart. Took notes, today, for Harvest. Keep thinking about what J said at supper: "a wonderful childhood." Why do I always assume that I did a bad job?

BLOOD ON THE HAWTHORNE

There was a storm in the night. Wind lashed the last leaves from the maple trees. They lie against the house, burying the pulpy stalks of foxglove, delphinium, snapdragons.

I stand in the back door, snapping the buttons of a fluorescent orange vest I've put on over my jacket. It's November—the first day of deer-hunting season. Our land is posted with yellow circles, indicating that permission is needed to hunt here. No one ever asks, so we assume we're safe on our own place. Still, bullets travel far, and for three weeks we go nowhere without orange vests, orange toques.

The air, knife-edged, slices down from the Arctic. As the sun shimmers up over the east ridge, I smell winter and sense the merciless clarity of the north. My little dog watches me intently. She's poised like a runner waiting for the pistol. I wave her away, impatiently.

೨೭

NOVEMBER I, 1994: *Lately, I wake to a sense of irritation, feel as if I'm always on edge. That's such an apt expression—neither here nor there. I'm never present. If I'm working in the studio, I think I should be writing or photographing. If I'm sitting at my desk or am out with my camera, I think I should be working in the studio. There's a quote taped over my packing desk that I once found both funny and admirable: "Bite off more than you can chew, and then chew like crazy." My hands have been trying to catch up with my mind's demands—they tear and ball paper, wind bubble wrap around vases, scribble invoices. Too much—too much of everything—have to figure out a way to cut down, slow down.*

Peter has stoked the furnace and started the day's work. Smoke rises from the chimney of the pottery studio. It blooms in the motionless air, thins, and then vanishes, like ink in water.

I set out down the drive. It's really more of a lane than a driveway, since it meanders between fields and meadows for a long while before it meets the valley road. Yet no one drives past our house—we're more likely to see a marsh hawk out the kitchen window than a car. Years ago, when manganese was mined from these hills, there were many farms, a school, a cheese factory; there was a post office in the front hall of our house. When we first came here, the old people told us how they used to come to our house for the mail. They spoke patiently, knowing that their memories were only stories to us, with a story's haze of unreality. As I walk down the lane, I try to imagine loads of ore coming up along the road, the creak of wagons, the clop of hooves, or children running down to the one-room schoolhouse that sits opposite the church, its white clapboards shining in the morning sun.

There's a particular stillness after a night of wind and rain. The land is inert, spent, like a woman after passion. There's not a breath of wind. I stop at the bridge, halfway down our lane. Wild mint flails in the silver-grey water. The brook runs insistently, its waters carrying away the remains of the storm.

Ten minutes ago Jake ran down this lane to catch the school bus. He was wearing fingerless gloves and a black raincoat that he bought for five dollars at the Sally Ann. His bookbag was slung over one shoulder, his tweed cap on backwards.

I stare down at the water. The past, like underwater weeds, pulls me into its tangled web. I'm seeing myself and Jake. He's three years old, it's winter, and he happily flings his red mitten into the river and watches it sail away. I'm furious. I rage at him. Remembering that, I press my fist to my mouth. It's not my remembered rage that sorrows me, but the way in which I shattered his happiness, his innocence. Year by year I tried to teach him how to curb his impulses, how to view the world. At three years old, he still saw so purely: *Red mitten: How will it look, flying through the air? Does it float? How fast will it travel? Look how it bounces, becomes a red spot in the grey running water!* I could have learned from a child how to regain my delight, but instead I was grumpy about having to buy another pair of mittens. Lost opportunities float in the unchangeable past. What other mistakes did I make? I walk on, mentally berating myself. Couldn't relax into motherhood. Had to keep working. Dragged Jake out to the studio in his playpen. Wore him in a backpack while I flung wood into the cellar. Those fights when he was in his earlier teens. Me: *It's our house too; we have rights. Get off the phone. I'm not your servant. Pick up your boots. Clean your room. Do your homework. Do. Do.*

No. Not. This way. Now! My mind frantic with the need to bend him, form him; and his resistance, strong as oak.

Lately I'm obsessed with thoughts that revolve endlessly; surfacing, sinking, surfacing. On the hawthorne bush, red berries hang like drops of blood.

I reach the end of our lane, meet the dirt road. Across the road is Mary's farm. I realize that it's Monday because she's hung her washing on the line. A minute ago she would have been standing at the window of her porch, absorbed in plucking clothespins from the basket on the sill, shaking out wet sheets, pinning up socks and underpants. Now she is gone, as Jake is gone, and only the blue plaid tea-towels remain to mark her passing. Beneath them, far beyond, I see the hazy blue lines of the hills, folding to the Bay of Fundy.

The gravelly crunch of my hiking boots is the only sound I hear as I head down the road towards the United Church. All the kids have been picked up by the bus, like flies sucked into a vacuum cleaner. I'm walking through empty air, and I wonder if there is no roar behind the tumult of human life. Perhaps its truth is silence: the silence of empty rooms, the spent stillness of land after storm.

A pickup truck passes, driven slowly by a stranger wearing a hunter-orange jacket. There's a gun-rack behind his head. He and another man are cruising, looking for deer. There are more strangers in our valley during hunting season than at any other time of the year. I resist my habit of raising my hand in a friendly wave. They feel like predators to me, invading our territory. I watch the truck pass the church and head up the steep side road towards the deer habitat on the hardwood ridges.

The hills have lost the brilliance they wore so proudly, the breathtaking leaf-fire of crimson, orange, and gold. Now the hardwoods—leafless, grey—are like a woman's face washed of makeup. I notice the evergreens as if for the first time. They were there all along, but now they step forward.

The valley houses are like boats that have been hauled out for winter. Their foundations are lapped with fir boughs. Gardens are tilled, mulched with straw. Next year's wood is piled for a year's seasoning. Storm windows, storm doors—everything's shut up tight. On the windless air, smoke rises straight and retains the shape of flues. It occurs to me that we spend our summers preparing for winter, and our winters longing for summer.

I've come a mile down the road, passing five houses, white-faced cows in pastures, and one barking dog. Now the valley ends, and the woods start. My impulse is to keep on going, striding as if towards some unknown but longed-for destination, breathing air that smells of cows and winter. But I force myself to turn and begin walking home.

I hear the crack of a gun. One shot, and then two others in rapid succession. The echoes shatter, flung back and forth between the hills. I stare up at the hillside, imagining a wide-eyed doe standing uncertainly in criss-crossing shadow. She flicks an ear, her heart pounds. She lifts a delicate hoof to take one more step.

After the gunshot, there's an expectant stillness. I stand listening, but can hear nothing but the splashing of the brooks.

❧

NOVEMBER 2, 1994: *There are seasons that have no names, at least not in my culture. They're edge seasons, thresholds, when the land seems to hang between what has just happened and what is yet to come.*

Inside the houses, there are preserves in pantries: Lady Ashburn pickles, chow, raspberry jam, apple jelly. Sacks of potatoes, smelling of earth, are bundled in dark cellars. Freezers are filled with beef, pork, and chicken. The chimney's been cleaned. Tractor tires clink with heavy chains. The calendar is about to change its bright photograph. Once again, we have prepared and worked hard for this moment. We hold the summer distilled—in wine bottles, in jam jars, in memory. The land is a husk of its summer self. There's nothing soft—no padding, no dross. Seed-pods are split, dry and gaping. The paper wasps' nests, pinioned on wild raspberry canes, gradually shred in the wind, and the petals of black-eyed Susans dry in wind-flung gestures. Over the winter, leaves will rot, slowly, the soft parts dissolving, with only an intricate lace of veins remaining by next spring. I walked, yesterday, down the valley, and all the way I felt, in my throat, the familiar ache: My son is leaving; my parents are growing old. Time passes, season after season after season. I can't save anything. I feel as if my life is a firefly clutched in a fist.

BIRTHDAY

Mid-November: Peter's birthday falls on a Sunday, and friends are coming for supper. We sleep late. For once I drift towards wakefulness like a child, aware of sleep's buoyant warmth and of waking's clarity; the two blend, gently. Peter's arm lies over my waist, his body cups mine. It's a windy, overcast day; branches of the birch tree scratch against the porch roof. I listen to the quiet of Jake's room. I wonder where he'll be at this time next year.

We linger over a birthday breakfast. I make scrambled eggs, set bread to toast on crumpled tinfoil laid on the wood stove. Jake goes out and feeds the flock of black silkies—small hens with sweeping tails—and throws hay onto the frozen soil for the horse and pony. He returns smelling of frost and manure. I pour the eggs into a frying pan. Peter's sitting at the table, examining his pile of gifts, eyebrows raised. We know he'll tease us by taking an intolerably long time to open each thing. Jake sits across from him.

"Open that one, Dad." He pokes a present with one finger, sending it over the edge of the table so Peter has to catch it.

Last year on Peter's birthday, Jake had to be prodded awake and was annoyed with us. This year he and his friend Corey found the perfect gift. Peter makes an elaborate show of opening it, commenting on the wrinkled used paper, trying to remember other presents it was used for, picking at the knot— and I see how someday, before too long, he and Jake will be friends. I long for it. I'm tired of mediating, brokering disputes.

"Nice, Jake," Peter says.

"What?" I move forward to see. In the paper are enormous dried pig's ears. Dog chews. These are entirely appropriate gifts for Peter, who loves costumes, has a set of horns made of moose-antler tips, and embarrasses Jake with outrageous hats. He holds the ears to his head.

"Oh, *nice*, Dad."

Peter goes to the dining room where there's a mirror.

❦

Peter and Jake are happy with each other all day. They ride their mountain bikes around the block, fifteen kilometres of dirt road through the industrial forest that spreads from our farm south and west: the woods have been recently clear-cut, or are halfway grown back, or are still dark and dense, ear-marked for harvest. I spend the morning making a birthday cake and setting the table. Then I work outside in the cold air, covering the flower gardens with hay, stacking kitchen wood in the back shed. At 3:30, when light is already draining from the sky, our friends arrive: Pete W, Judith, and their daughter, Maya. We've been family friends for years. Their son is already away at university, and Maya will leave soon. We stand in the driveway, preparing to set out for a quick walk before supper. Peter and Pete W exchange rude guy comments pertaining to age and physical capabilities. Judith is tiny, tough, sparrow-boned: she wears a black ankle-length wool coat, mittens, and a long scarf wound around her neck, covering her mouth and nose.

"Oh, Mum. You're such a baby," Maya says. She and Jake are hatless, bare-handed. They stride fast, side by side.

When they were little, Judith and I remind each other, we'd take long family hikes at Fundy Park and sometimes, by the end of the day, they'd lag behind, whining.

We go up across the fields and through the woods, circling round behind the ravine and stopping at the edge of its eighty-foot cliff to look back at our farm, toy-sized. Dusk falls as we descend through the leafless hardwoods, and we're pink-cheeked when we arrive back at the house. In the hall we unwind scarves, unlace boots. Peter carries in stove wood, and Pete W heads for the pantry, where he takes beer bottles from the refrigerator. I cook rice and, at the last minute, sear scallops in garlic butter.

At the dining-room table we banter in the way of old friends, yet even as I tease, question, exclaim, I'm wondering if everyone else feels as I do: that the largest part of myself remains hidden behind my smiling face; that my public self is an integument, wearing thin. Words I'd like to say press, quiver, and remain unspoken. I flick the ash from the wick of a guttering candle flame. We're reminding Maya of the time she mooned us, in a ski condominium in Maine.

"I never did."

"And we"—I grin at Judith—"changed in the parking lot."

Forty-six candles on the cake: one to grow on. The year before my grandfather died, my grandmother wished, as she blew out the candles on her birthday cake, that we would all still be together on the next birthday. Afterwards, she told this story whenever someone was presented with a birthday cake, until my mother found ways to forestall her.

Peter blows the candles. Jake and Maya are watching. They're like cats, present but poised, as if ready to spring away. We grown-ups are jolly—joyful, silly, a merriment slightly forced—as if we're all aware of our fraying connection.

❧

After they leave, Jake yawns, feeling the effect of so much fresh air, and goes up to his room early. Peter is absorbed with a birthday book. I sit in the kitchen, where the stove fire is making feeble snaps, slowly dying. I can see my reflection in the window as I phone my brother in Rhode Island. He's a professional guitarist. He and his wife, a mandolinist, have produced many CDs. Like Peter with his exhibitions, they make me feel inadequate. I'm the one member of the family who has produced nothing. *Nothing to show, thus a failure.*

"Hi, Mark."

"Hey!"

I tell him about the good day we've just had. He responds, a yearning note in his voice. He loves our northern farm. We perceive each other's lives with a degree of romance.

"I feel . . ." It's hard. We don't talk about feelings. We've been taught to keep them to ourselves.

Lately childhood memories spin in my mind. I want to make them come alive, like objects stored in boxes: take them out, dust them off, put them to use. Who were they, really, those remote, remembered people: grandparents, great-aunts, teachers? The gigantic parents of infancy? I pull memories towards me, dim as faded sketches.

"Do you remember the time Mum told us that Dad had been in a car accident? It was a freezing cold night in winter. You and I were in the living room. I can see the black, frosted windowpanes. She was terrified."

"No," he says. He's a kind person and doesn't like to disagree. But that is not how it was. "He wasn't in an accident. He was just late."

"But I was terrified. I cried and cried. I had a recurrent dream, for years, that he was killed."

"*Really.*"

We exchange other stories. He explores his memories hesitantly, like a person speaking in a foreign language.

Can he explain a memory of fire sirens in the night? The tattooed man in the guest-room bed? He's surprised by my questions. Memory has not yet haunted him, even though he's older than I am. He's so busy, engaged in life. Their children are younger than Jake. He doesn't seem to know what it's like to be approaching change, to feel stopped or paused.

"This is what I really want to know."

"Okay, what."

"Why do you play the guitar?"

He's silent. He is not self-analytical.

"Is it because you need to practise for performances?"

"No," he says instantly. He sounds shocked. "Not at all. I hear music in my head, constantly. I go around all day with music in my head. I play because I have to. I *have* to. If I can't sleep, I get up and go down to the living room. I put on that lamp with the pink shade. It makes a low, soft light. I make tea. Sometimes I sit for hours playing quietly. So I won't wake the family."

"What do you play?"

"Anything. Something we're working on. Something I'm making up."

When he plays, his face is remote with concentration. His mouth is taut, stern, but his eyes are compassionate.

After we say goodbye, I sit in the chair by the stove. His guitar is his voice. Music is not what he does: it is who he is.

❧

NOVEMBER 16, 1994: *P's birthday yesterday. A good day. I need to find clarity inside myself. I need to stop allowing other people, or circumstances, to set my agenda. I must not care about what people think—either of me or of what I do. I need to find the strength to do what I want to do. I am in the habit of smothering myself, hiding, as if who I am is somehow shameful. I thought, after talking to my brother last night: I don't have to write. No one is making me. No one cares. And this was an enormous relief to me. Then, this morning, when I came to my desk I felt open, receptive, as if life, words, could pour through me. I wrote because I had to— because I wanted to.*

STONY FINGERS

Winter's stony fingers tighten. Fields are brown, skies leaden. At five o'clock in the afternoon, on November 31st, there's no sunset, simply an intensifying darkness. I stand in the lane and look back at the house. Lighted, framed by the maples, it seems warm, flickering, and self-contained, like a Hallowe'en pumpkin.

The presence of winter binds the landscape, a brooding tension holding ice to pebble, moss to bark, cold to stillness. Beneath its skirting of ice, the brook is muffled and makes a hollow knocking. Dusk-dark fields roll up to paler sky; over my head, twig and branch offer no shelter.

I could go into the house, to Peter and Jake, to dog and cats, to music, light, and the evening news. But I stand in the cold, my hands by my sides, mittened, like the earth, whose coiling and wrapping is complete. Twigs and the movement of air make a thin whistle, a rushing that rises and subsides, rises again and gathers into a small roar, then settles tentatively, like a cat's tail. I smell snow on the air. Then I see flakes in the light over the back door. The wind rises, and the trees begin their winter moan. I look out over the fields, claimed, now, by wind, snow, and darkness. I walk back to the house and find the back step already covered with a fluff of crystals.

After supper I go out to the barn to do the chores. When I'm done, I sit on the milking platform we built when we had goats. The weather forecaster has announced a winter storm. It's begun—what we used to call, in Jake's childhood, "the season of the white witch." We call our valley "the white witch's kingdom" because it is high above sea level and has deeper, longer-lasting snow—or so it seems to us—than anywhere else. The wind builds like a wave, crashes against the old walls: spent, its remnants moan at corners, suck at cracks. It's a snow-wind, dancing with another element, alive with icy tappings, its whirling path described by drifts.

I feel the animal warmth, the animal peace. The barn smells of timothy and red top, of dried daisy heads. The hens sit side by side on a manure-encrusted pole. Lids slide up and down over their reptilian eyes. One makes a quiet *chirr*, stretches her neck, lifts her wings, and jumps off her perch with a thump. Snow sifts under the door and makes a tiny, sinuous drift. It finds its way through cracks in the walls and outlines every nailhead, every timber, every piece of hay. Even the frozen sawdust on the chicken-pen floor is white. The horse and pony, thick coated, are oblivious to the snow that fills the groove of their spines, that drips from their fetlocks. Their jaws grind steadily. They're content, curious—their ears prick forward. They listen, like me, to the winter that declares itself, like a person returning from exile.

I lean back against the cold wall and fold my arms across my chest. I listen to the mare's steady munching, the rustling of hay as the saggy-backed pony digs vigorously with her muzzle. Flakes tick against the windowpanes. Timbers shift and creak. A loose sheet of steel bangs on the roof. My shoulders relax. I'm in a ship, sailing through a storm with animals who are not afraid, who do not imagine disaster, who trust the comforts that sustain them.

I go into my black mare's stall, put my arms around her neck, and lay my cheek against her mane. She flicks an ear backward. I absorb her calm, like a flush of wine to the blood. I close my eyes and let my arms go limp as they circle her neck.

$\approx$

The next morning it's still snowing. The radio announces school cancellations. Jake burrows into his pillow and hauls his quilt over his head. Peter and I go up into the fields on our cross-country skis. We ski up along the brook to the sauna. It no longer looks abandoned but stands straight and tidy under a softening shawl of snow. Snow gathers on the rungs of the ladder, on the pile of lumber. The jacks supporting the timbers are already buried.

"Have to bring a tarp up, cover this wood." Peter brushes snow from the two-by-fours with a gloved hand.

"We can work up here for a while, still," I say. But not for much longer. Mid-winter will put the project on hold.

We ski up an old woods road through firs and birch and then herringbone up a steep meadow. At the top we push through the hedgerow and stand side by side, looking down the valley. Snowflakes hang on my eyelashes. The wind has died and the snow wavers down quietly, brushing the landscape, making it dim and obscure. The opposite hills are pale, their spruce trees grey-green. The houses lose importance, their roofs humped with snow like boulders.

The empty fields of November, frozen, with ragged wildflowers, are transformed. Each flake of snow holds the possibility of iridescence. Millions of prisms lie dormant on this hushed morning, waiting for the sun to quicken their spectrums.

We follow a hedgerow up along one side of a field, heading towards the forest. A trail of coyote tracks emerges from the trees. The tracks are neat, oval, as evenly spaced as links in a chain. They parallel the hedgerow, loop across the field, and vanish in the whiteness where field meets snow-sky.

I lean on my poles. My eyes follow the coyote's trail. He would rather, I think, have trotted into the heart of winter in total obscurity, like a ship vanishing into fog. He had no need or desire to leave any trace of his passing.

WINTER

BLUE SHADOWS

The windows are frost-blind. Rooms are filled with light. I walk from window to window looking for the hills, the barn, the snow-laden maples, but all I see on these December mornings is the windowpanes' world: needle crystals and blue frost ferns, delicate as wing-tips brushed on snow.

As the sun rises, the icy windows glitter with the minute shifting of the sun's rays. The cats seek pentagons of sunlight on the pine floor. They sprawl like otters, industriously licking the white fur of their bellies. I crouch in a chair, prop my feet on its rungs, and warm my hands on a mug of steaming coffee. I stare at the blind, sparkling south window.

We're in a hiatus between working cycles. We've taken our pottery to the Toronto show; we've shipped our orders. Out in the studio the kilns stand with their lids open, nothing inside but fire brick and electrical coil. Peter's Kevlar mitts, his leather apron and welder's shirt, his air-supplied respirator with its coil of hose, his trash cans of smoke-blackened sawdust—all these elements of his raku dance lie like ballet slippers on a shelf. Our employees are laid off until mid-January. In my study, my slides are filed and my desk is bare.

❧

71

DECEMBER 14, 1994: *I feel myself sliding sideways, drifting through days not striped by the hard sections of time but patterned by darkness and light, by evening shadow and blue moon-glimmer in window frost, by sunrise that shatters snow and lifts in the first purl of chimney smoke. The days evolve, blend one into the next. I forget whether it's Friday or Tuesday.*

I sip my coffee and ponder Christmas. I long for its images to quicken me, the way the ice crystals make magic with morning light. I close my eyes to visualize the holiday. *Wreath, stollen, spiced wine. Candlelight on the faces of friends. Secrets buried in bureau drawers. Wood stove snapping, flour on my jeans. Spruce tree in the living room. Family arriving.* I try to see these memories and imaginings as they've always been—shining fragments of a numinous moment. But they're scattered in my mind's landscape like masks with empty eyeholes.

I turn towards the table, set down my mug, and slide my fingers into my hair. Lately, everything is a battle. I had a wave of rage when we unloaded the truck: cartons of pots brought back, unsold, from the Toronto show.

DECEMBER 15, 1994: *I am so sick of handling* PRODUCT. *My moods go up and down. I have to make it clear to myself where I should focus my energies. Sometimes life seems pointless.*

Snow came early this year.

Our ski track loops up the big hill, makes a blue chain pattern that vanishes beneath the spruce trees. By the back door, when chickadees land on the honeysuckle, handfuls of snow shake loose. The maples at the bottom of the lawn are a maze of criss-crossing black and white lines, every twig outlined with snow. When the sun rises, the trees are like a line of dancers, strength and delicacy balanced. I open the barn door, and the horse and pony gallop out, snow-glitter at their hooves, their muzzles spiked with frost.

Along the north side of the house, drifts cover the windows; the dining room is dimmed by cold, iceberg light. In the kitchen and the living room, however, the light is lively: frost-ferns on the windows shimmer as the sun travels over the southern hills.

These are the unbalanced days, when night, like snow, claims the land. As the snow deepens—burying raspberry canes, concealing the brooks—darkness falls earlier and stays longer. In the morning Jake goes down the drive to wait for the bus just as first light touches the ridge. By four o'clock in the afternoon, twilight is already gathering in blue shadows around the studio, under lilac bushes, in the lee of riverbanks.

One day I ski up the hill to watch the sunset. At the top of the big field I kick-turn to face down the valley. I lean forward on my poles. My eyelashes are frozen, and my cheeks hold the flushed light of the dying sun. Down the valley it reflects in windows, making it appear as though each house burns from within.

There's not a whisper of sound. The only movement is the prism-quiver of snow crystals. They are like millions of tiny, heatless fires, each flake reflecting the sun's descent as the earth rolls us away from its star and turns towards the black universe. The sun is far in the southwest; I watch it sinking into the chalice of the hills. Next week will be the winter solstice: the shortest day of the year and the longest night. As cold dusk rises around me, I ponder sun-worshippers such as the North American Hopi. As the winter sun travelled farther and farther south, giving less light and less warmth, dwindling in power, they were uncertain whether it would return. With stones, sticks, and red paint, with chants and cries, with the potency of fear couched in ceremony, they implored it to return.

I pull my neck warmer over my nose. *I know it's going to return. My fear is different. One day the people I love will not be here to greet it.*

It's minus 24 Celsius. I try to hear something, anything, just to know that I'm not deaf. But there is no sound. Darkness creeps from the hedgerows, spreads from the barns and the pastures, as steady in its rising as the sun is swift in its setting. I ball my cold hands into fists inside my mittens. My life is speeding past, tipping me towards death. Grandparents, aunts, and uncles are gone: the fabric of my childhood has been torn into bits and is drifting, tattered, on the winds of memory. I have been weaving a new fabric with such care and energy: making a family, a home. Peter and I built porches, dug gardens, found friends, made a business. We painted walls, built cupboards, bought couches, and filled our rooms with pottery, paintings, braids of garlic, red geraniums. I made a world for Jake, thinking of the memories he'd have as I hung baby clothes on a wooden rack by the stove; as I made applesauce or baked cookies; as I watched Peter hang a mobile of bright, stuffed fish over his cradle. I made him a squirrel costume, and I watched with trepidation as his sturdy little body walked away, going to Cub Scouts or swimming lessons or kindergarten. I snuggled on the couch with one arm around him, entering the world of picture books, talking bears, flying horses. Now, I sense dissolution. It rises like dusk, obliterating light. I see this life we've made vanishing, like all the ones that have preceded ours.

The sky turns cobalt. Stars prick out over the barn. The moon is gibbous, between first quarter and full, and hangs high in the east, translucent as a jellyfish. It's the precise instant between day and night when darkness softens the sky, but the dying light still reddens bark and gleams on spruce needles. A chickadee flies over the flushed snow and drops into a pine tree.

I push off. My narrow skis waver, find the track, then slide surely, with gathering speed. I feel a sudden, reckless energy that is like making a bonfire in the night and waving my arms at the unblinking yellow eyes that creep forward. *Get away, stupid thoughts! Leave me in peace.* Tomorrow I'll make a wreath. I'll begin my Christmas baking. I'll get Peter to help me hang white lights on the birch tree and light the copse where the birdfeeders hang. Next week we'll cut our tree. *Christmas.* In the word's sibilance, I hear the magic of light reflected in glass, interiors laid upon the night, the lacing of lives with rituals repeated. The word flames and crackles, lifting my spirits as I ski down into the dark valley.

♦

DECEMBER 17, 1994: *It is cold, windy, and snowing. Quite dark at 4:10. I'm in my office listening to music, flipping through the pages of my finished manuscript, looking at slides on my light table, wondering what would happen if I finally had the courage to channel my energy into my own work. I spend so much of my time on other things, especially the business. Right now my gorge rises even at the thought of setting foot in the studio, yet the idea of hiring someone to do my work— packing, keeping track of orders—scares me. There's something that I'm afraid to give up.*

CHRISTMAS RITES

My parents' calendar taught me to visualize time. It was sent to them by their insurance company and hung on the wall over the telephone table. Every month there was a different Currier and Ives painting of nineteenth-century people going on outings. They wore furs in winter, enormous straw hats in summer. Horses with tiny heads and long necks pulled sleighs or carriages: their eyes, white-rimmed, rolled backwards as if terrified by the long-handled whips brandished by drivers. In my child's mind, a year was made of twelve large squares; each of these squares was divided into four rows of smaller squares. Time, and its passing, was obscurely related to frightened horses. My life would be a progression of calendar pages, flipping over and over until, finally, the pages ended.

My parents also taught me how to make wreaths—circles, round, whole, without beginning or end.

There's only one more week of school. I stand on tiptoe and hold Jake's shoulder while I plant a kiss on his cheek. He crosses the snowy lawn, leaping into yesterday's tracks, and then strides sure-footed down the icy lane.

After breakfast Peter and I ski up to the woods to cut fir boughs. We haul the toboggan. When we reach the top of the hill, we push between spruce and fir, their branches bent by snow loads. Snow gathers in the folds of our jackets without melting. As the Swede saw ratchets the quiet, essence of fir sharpens the air: sap-drenched, raw, bracing. Peter throws me branches curved like feathers, and I nest them on the toboggan, cupping one over the other and securing them with baling twine. We ski back down, snow in our faces, and carry scratchy armloads of boughs into the kitchen. Ice melts along their spines; wet needles speckle the floor.

I sit cross-legged amid wool mittens and kicked-off boots. Bending long, supple branches around a masonite ring, I secure them with wire and then tuck tips, one under the next. Dust motes and cat hairs spin in the sunlight. The wild resinous smell of the forest fills the kitchen. Around and around I tuck the fir tips, making a seamless circle, its framework hidden. My hands snip, tuck, poke, grip.

When it's done, I take the wreath outside and hang it from a rusty nail on the back door. The door is yellow, its paint scratched and dented, its latch shiny from a century of thumbs and fingers. I stand back, squinting in the snow-brilliant light. The white farmhouse is transformed. Here it sits in the midst of snowy fields—clapboards, shingles, steel roof, brick chimney—and it becomes a gift. The wreath is like ribbon on a package.

Going back inside, I slide my mitten into the door latch. Just for a minute I lay my other hand on the wreath. Its inner curve is strong as a horse's neck. It begins, the rhythm of ritual running like a cross-tide over the short days.

❧

DECEMBER 18, 1994: *Wrapped Christmas presents all afternoon. J and two friends came over. They skied up to the ravine, then came in and made freeze-dried soup that they'd brought. I came into the living room to find all three guys upside-down on the couch, bums in the air, feet hanging over their heads, arms crossed, amicably chatting. Went to the café tonight—heard a quartet of women singers from Moncton and saw many friends. Everyone sang carols and drank beer. Coming home, there were brilliant stars over the dark valley and Christmas lights like beacons for lost travellers.*

❧

It's snowing, and the hills are soft grey-green. Across the meadow, our neighbour's house is obscured, and the alders are like smudged pencil drawings. The world draws in to what is close: flakes spinning down, loose and wavering on the air, and the yellow-billed grosbeaks bright as fruit on the branches of the poplar. Time shifts subtly, the white light growing darker, gently, as the day passes.

The day passes on its own terms, connected only to its

context. I'm baking: Christmas cookies, stollens, and sweet breads. I work at the maple-wood table facing the stove and the east window. The table is like any place of work where one element is combined with another to make real what has been imagined: a painter's studio, a jeweller's bench. There are bowls filled with almonds and walnuts, piles of candied fruit, currants soaking in hot water, pieces of paper with handwritten recipes, wooden spoons, a crock of flour. Bits of candied citron stick to the edge of a paring knife. A raku bowl is filled with white flour freckled with mace and cardamom. Kneading a loaf, the heels of my hands feel hidden treasures inside the dough: cherries, nuts, lemon peel.

I made a fire in the wood stove this morning. I'm using an electric oven as well, but I love the sound of the wood stove— its tickings, hissings, high-pitched whingings. I want the kettle to wheeze quietly all day. I want some of my cookies to be unevenly baked, crisper on the firebox side and infused with a cindery taste.

I feel as quiet as the white snow-light that pervades the house. My mind is stilled, smoothed, like a messy yard blanketed by snow. I'm grounded by what I'm doing. The palms of my hands move effortlessly; I'm the Oscar Peterson of flour-kneading. My body knows the choreography of this dance—a pinch rather than a measured spoon; set the timer while passing the stove; glance outside at the birds; wipe floury hands on jeans; slide out pans of bread, sheets of cookies.

The smell of yeast and nutmeg rises through the house and triggers memory. Thirty years ago my mother spent December days doing just what I'm doing. It was a Connecticut winter, in the

1950s, but the same thin sunlight slanted through the window-panes. I was five years old, and I pressed these very same aluminum cookie cutters into dough made from the very same recipe that I use today. The cookies are shaped like wild things—trees, stars, rabbits, reindeer, half-moons. They taste of butter and mace. They're toasty brown. It's my mother's bread recipe as well. Four round loaves lie on the kitchen table, cinnamon and cherries breaking through their crusts. As I sprinkle icing sugar over them, I feel like a priestess or a witch, adding a pinch of sacred hazel to some potent brew. Each single element is part of something larger.

There is no other time in the year when I could spend all day in the kitchen combining flour and currants, music, fir boughs and fire, and feel so centred, knowing that this is exactly what I'm supposed to be doing. I prop myself in the door frame of the living room, holding a mug of coffee and looking at the place where we'll put the tree later this evening.

Just before sunset we ski up to get the tree. We've already chosen it, to avoid the dreadful family arguments we used to have a few years ago.

In the blue shadows it stands as still and snow-laden as all the others. Already, Jake and I feel remorse. Neither of us wants to do the actual cutting, so Peter takes off his skis and kneels in the snow. I knock snow off the branches with my ski pole and push against the trunk as he saws, feeling the strange moment when the tree is no longer elastic and tensile but falls forward into the air.

Going back down the hill, we ski into the sunset, snow flying up around us. Jake hauls the tree on the toboggan. The moon rises. Grown from its shell-like fragility to a commanding fullness, it pulses up behind the spruce trees and slides blue-silver into the sky.

When we arrive at the house, there are stars over the barn and the cats are waiting for us, twitchy-tailed. We drag the tree into the house. Its presence transforms the hall, the kitchen, and the dining room as it passes through. It sheds bark, resin, needles, and a forest essence comprising the tree's long communion with wind, earth, and sun. In the cold, icy fragrance is a sense of darkness and silence. We'll sweep up later. Clutter is part of the process. The couch is swivelled out of place, branch tips laid on its cushions. The floor is strewn with lopsided shoeboxes: out of them we lift glass balls, strands of red and silver beads, starched embroidered stars. The room smells of the cranberry-popcorn chains I loop from branch to branch. Peter stands on a chair and hangs his favourite ornament, a plastic banana, from the tree's tip. Jake and I object, as always, but he insists it's a crescent moon. "Okay, that's enough decoration," says Jake, finally. We go around the house, turning off lights so we can see how the tree reflects in the glass doors of the sunroom, how its lights gleam on the cranberries and fold in the earlobe curves of popcorn.

It lives in me all year—the memory of this moment when the tree becomes a symbol with a power out of all proportion to its elements. I lie on the couch, arms crossed behind my head. The room smells of balsam, the taste of Christmas when I nibble a fir needle in summer. I think of the ancient peoples who performed such rituals of transformation, making one thing imitate another to gain control over what they feared.

Jake and I put on our coats and go out onto the lawn. We stand under the maples and look back at the house. Without its lights, the house loses its inner energy. It's simply a square box. In the moonlight I can imagine it abandoned and empty. Only one window is lighted by the Christmas tree, which sparkles cold as starlight, but I can also see the firelike warmth of its glistening red balls. It shines across the fields, deeply familiar, profoundly human, framed by the window—as if you could put hope in a box, hold it steady, make it visible.

THE HUMBLED MOON

DECEMBER 20, 1994: *I'm trying to figure out the moon. Sometimes I notice a crescent moon, almost invisible in the daytime sky. Then it's a coin that vanishes in the west as the sun rises, or a majestic globe that comes up over the eastern ridge just when the sun is setting. Sometimes it's nowhere to be found, and then I search the sky, wondering in what aspect it will appear next. I read how the North American Indians named the monthly moons "The Moon of the Ripening Strawberries," "The Moon of the Laying Geese," "The Moon of the Stirring of the Racoons after Hibernation," "The Moon of the Arrival of Eagles." Or they called the moon back, every month, when it briefly passed between the earth and the sun and showed its shadowed face. They shouted encouragement, held their arms outspread.*

During the last Ice Age, people carved notches on bones to record the lunar months.

The moon seems capricious, yet it circles the earth faithfully every month, its patterns making the tides that strand fishing boats on the Fundy mud and then surge back, foam-edged, to lift them up again. It dances across the sky in a lovely cycle—new, to first quarter, to full, to last quarter, to new—marking the passage of nights, sleeps, and seasons. Stars, too, keep their relation to one another and make patterns within a greater pattern, wheeling, turning—summer stars, winter stars.

I long to understand time as rhythm. I wonder if my obsession with how it races past is related to the ancient dread of powerlessness, fearing the sun's winter retreat, eclipses, or the moon's wane. Life seems meaningless, yet I begin to see how things that recur over and over again—Christmas, gardens, moon cycles—steady me.

❧

On December 23, Peter and Jake leave after supper to pick up Peter's brother, Andy, at the airport. It's an hour's drive each way. I watch the tail lights as the car turns at the end of the lane, passes Mary's house, and goes down past the church. The red lights dwindle and become part of the night.

I work a log into the firebox of the kitchen stove and push the kettle to the back burner. I put on my long wool coat, wrap a scarf around my neck, and step out into the cold air, heading over to the church for the special service held on the last Sunday before Christmas. As I walk up the road, I hear the mournful reediness of the pump organ. The church shines against the night sky: its windows are starred with electric candles, and real candles flicker in glass jars twisted into snow along the path.

I walk up the steps and go inside. The big box wood stove has been fired up since noon, and the church, with its varnished wood walls, is hot. Marjorie, in her eighties, sits behind the pump organ, peering at music through the bottom of her glasses. There's a Christmas tree with red ribbons tied on the ends of its branches. The electric candles in the windowsills give the little church a soft radiance. There are many children at this service. The minister is ushering them to the front pews.

I sit by one of the tall, narrow windows. Across the meadow I can see our house, its Christmas tree like a tiny star shining in the moonlit valley.

Sue and her husband and two teenage boys sit in the pew behind me. She pats me on the shoulder. She wears a maroon wool dress coat with a Christmas corsage of holly. "Have Peter and Jake gone to get Andy?" she asks.

I love the way Sue knows about our lives. It makes me feel part of the community. It's the way it is supposed to be in this valley. Who has a bad knee, whose mother-in-law has cancer, whose relatives are coming for Christmas: everyone knows and cares. Men I'm accustomed to seeing in jackets and work pants wear ties and sports jackets beneath winter parkas. People smile at one another, acknowledging the heat as they unzip jackets, work at buttons, turn to lay their coats over the pews.

The minister suggests it is time for the passing of the peace. We all stand and leave our pews. Every single person shakes hands with every single other person, like clinking glasses at a toast. "Merry Christmas, Merry Christmas." Any grievances are set aside. Everyone's eyes touch. The children are taught to participate. They are told names and expected to repeat them.

The minister raises his arms. His sleeves spread forward like wings as he grips either side of the pulpit and bows his head. The congregation settles into a different kind of quiet, like leaves floating down when the wind suddenly dies.

He's a warm-hearted man. When he says, "Let us pray," I feel as if he is gathering words to speak to someone he loves and trusts, and who is actually listening.

I don't often attend church, and I recognize a familiar sense both of detachment and yearning. The God whom he addresses is here for me, I realize, in the elements that have come together in this building—the sound of the fire, ticking; the knocking of children's feet against the pews; the way people who all live within ten minutes' walk from one another sit, patiently, listening; the peace that calms my mind.

We stand and sing, and we watch the children light the last candle of Advent. We sing "Happy Birthday" to Jesus.

"Is it really Jesus' birthday?" a child whispers.

"Yes. Shh."

"I thought Jesus was *dead*."

People pass amused glances. The child's mother presses her forefinger to her lips, shakes her head. The minister comes down from the pulpit and sits in a chair; the children cluster around him as he tells the Christmas story. We sing the last carol, "Joy to the World." A buzz of talk rises the instant the service is over. People linger in the aisle, shuffle forward, reach to pat a shoulder, shake a hand, ruffle hair. Amy and Alyson's father hands a candy cane to everyone. Many people ask for Peter and Jake. I feel as if, for once, I'm a bird in a flock. My hands have felt the bones of twenty other hands. I've been pulled into a few hugs, smelled clean hair, felt the scratch of men's cheeks.

I stand on the path between the candles in their glass jars. It's minus 18 and I pull a neck warmer over my nose and a toque as far down as it will go, so only my eyes are exposed. People wave, call goodbyes, spilling out of the church and hurrying to the warmth of their cars. I wave my mittened hand at Sue and walk away down the road, leaving behind the square of light falling from the door as the last people to leave shake hands with the minister, and boys jump lopsidedly over the candles in the snow. Engines rev, voices call and laugh. By the time I reach Mary's house, only a few cars are left at the church, someone is extinguishing its lights, and all I can hear is the crunching squeak of snow under my boots.

I turn down our lane, cross the bridge, reach the row of maples. All around me snow-covered fields unfold under the moon, soft wings laid over the earth's skeleton. They glisten, repellant and alluring as a moonlit room. The moon hangs in the centre of the eastern sky as though it has finally reached a place where it fits best, like an egg in the palm of your hand. It's the moon of children's books, perfectly round, perfectly centred.

I stop walking and stare at the sky. Cold penetrates my coat.

There's a black smudge on the side of the moon. It's unsettling, like a bruise on a child's face. It's a puzzling tarnish, a shadow where no shadow should be.

86

I go into the house. The fire has burned down to coals; I lift the stove lid and work in a few sticks of wood. All the lights are off except the ones on the Christmas tree and the window candles. I sit in the sunroom and watch the moon through binoculars. The smudge has grown and defined itself into a curving line. I realize with amazement that what I'm seeing is the earth's shadow cast upon the moon. The curving line is the earth's rim. *This is what my planet looks like!* It's like catching sight of yourself in a mirror for the first time. We are creatures inhabiting a body we can't see.

I watch the umbra slide across the moon as the earth looms between moon and sun. The umbra is a smoke-red veil; it seeps into the silver like blood in water. The fields darken, gradually, as the snow crystals cease to glitter. The great shadow eliminates all other shadows. Slowly, the black reflections on the snow grow pale, until nothing is luminous and the world seems lifeless, without dimension.

I put down the binoculars, shrug into my parka, and go outside. It's so cold that the air cuts my throat, stabs my lungs. I stare at the place in the sky where the moon hung only moments ago. Now it's merely a dusky place in the blackness. The stars, meanwhile, grow more brilliant. The displacement has its passionless consequences.

In the crushing cold I sense the relentless passage not of time but of repetition; the circling of the planets, the logic of interstellar mathematics. Of what consequence is my caring? Of what use is the glimmer of moonlight, the deceptive depth of shadow? Inside myself I hear both the silence of the universe and the noise of life. And I stand between.

The temperature is dropping, and I feel my body heat failing. I stare at the humbled moon, or the place in the sky where I know it is. If I looked away, I might not find it again, like losing track of a high-flying hawk. The stars flash—red, green, blue. A branch cracks. The universe bends close, and its vast oblivion creeps into me.

Head tipped back, hands in armpits, I remember a dream. Peter and I are in a boat with white sails. We are going away, and Jake is staying behind. I'm compelled by the urgent need to speak to Jake. I tell him he must pay the bills. I tell him I've signed the cheques. I take a breath to tell him more, to tell him everything. I have only one more instant, and I wonder if I've taught him all he needs to know. And then I let him go.

It is we who sail away, and he who stays home. And we navigate, like the moon, by the night's logic.

Headlights are coming along the driveway. At the maples, the car pauses so Andy can jump out. He runs towards me, his feet slipping in the unaccustomed snow. We meet, our arms circling each other, even as, in the sky, the earth moves on and the moon gradually reinstates herself, serene goddess of the night. Once again the fields glitter. Jake goes into the house, turns on the kitchen light. Golden squares fall from the window and checker the snow.

FIELD MOUSE

Rain comes at the tail end of the holiday. Now, in early January, the fields are brown, save for islands of snow, and there's ice in the low-lying meadow.

Christmas vanished as easily as the snow. One minute it surrounded me, dancing in all the corners of the house. Then Andy went down the boot hall carrying his suitcase, and I waved as he and Peter drove away. Jake trudged down the lane to wait for the school bus. The house was empty.

❧

JANUARY 5, 1995: *Every year, when I take down the tree, the decorations lose their magic, turn back to ordinary and tatty objects— scratched glass balls, wrinkled origami birds. As the holiday fades and the snow melts, I lose my sense of the sparkly excitement of winter. I feel as dull as the dead grass, and I'm touched with a familiar dread. What is real and what is artifice? To what extent do I create my life? What would happen if I stopped planting, baking, making? What would be left of me if I did nothing? I am tired of myself. The house feels hollow, and Jake is irritable. He resists my questions about school, friends, plans. He seems remote. He's withdrawing from us, psychologically. I realize this is a necessary process, but it feels like rejection. Peter wonders out loud why we live here. He bears more of the burden of fighting winter and property maintenance than I do. We argue. It's a cyclical discussion, comes up every January. I can't admit that there are things we gave up to live here. Nowhere is perfect, I insist. There's always a price to pay. Is he willing to give up the beauty of this place in*

*winter—skiing, sunsets, skating, and bonfires—for slushy streets, just
so we can attend plays and concerts, have more contact with other
artists? He's hungry for these things and so am I, although I don't dare
admit it to him. He's putting off going out to the studio and beginning
another year's work cycle. We're facing the long northern winter without another celebration, at least until the confusing ceremony of Easter.*

*Today I found my mind roving continually over all the things I
might have done with my life. I decided that it's time to stop doing this.
Instead of being obsessed with who I am not, I need to start seeing, and
liking, who I am.*

I need to send out my manuscript.

ෙ

On a weekday morning there's cloud cover, and the light, seeping into the kitchen, makes no shadows, only a metallic gleam
on the edge of eggs, teakettle, and the smooth arms of the rocking chair.

Peter has gone to the studio, and I'll follow after washing the
breakfast dishes, sweeping the floor, making phone calls. The
sound of arguing voices issues from the radio. I pick up a pottery cereal bowl in one hand and an egg cup in the other. Egg
shells spill. I put down bowl and egg cup, reach for the broom.
On the radio, raucous music replaces the voices. My planned
tasks slither in my mind like the pieces of a jigsaw puzzle. I
imagine myself choosing one piece, then searching, with frustra-
tion, for another.

I put back the broom and turn off the radio. I'm standing in
an empty house surrounded by empty fields. *Talk, organize,*

90

laugh, soothe. It's all evasion—a way to keep myself weightless and flying. There seems to be no heft to my days, no substance. The busier I am, the faster the days pass. I'm speeding through life like a bullet: nothing stops me; nothing sets me drifting, floating.

I go into the hall and pull on winter layers: mittens, toque, felt-lined boots. I dress slowly, hampered by a sense of work to be done: making a living. Yet I am torn by the sensation that something is being neglected and will fade away if I don't find it.

The sky broods like a hen, gathering clouds, hatching snow. I can smell the winter grass. Even though it's hollow-stemmed, wisping through the snow-patches, it is rooted, and there's still some growing earthiness in it. My feet tip over the frozen ruts of the lane leading towards the pond. It occurs to me that I'm walking on this dirt road the same way I've been living my life: stumbling along simply because it leads to an imaginable destination, picturing in my mind what I'm going to do next rather than seeing what's in front of me. I step off the path and climb over the rusty barbed-wire fence into the meadow. I punch through the shell of my preoccupations, make myself see. There's the brook with its red-skinned alders, snaking through a swale. Ice amplifies its low, steady burble, hollow as a voice speaking into a box. The winter colours are like a sun-faded quilt: yellow-barked willows, brown grass, bone-white raspberry canes.

In the absence of motivation, I'm drawn to the brook simply because it seems like the only thing besides myself that's alive in the naked land. I shoulder into the alders that grow on its banks. On their trunks are skirts of ice, remnants of a higher water level, their edges blunt, paddle-shaped. They blink—black, white, black, white—as water pulses close beneath.

I stand in the alders, wondering who I've become. Taking apart the magic of Christmas exposes the charlatan I sense myself to be. I don't believe in the person I present to the world. My smile has become too bright, like an expiring bulb. Some days I feel like the ice my boots have been crunching through. I'm easily broken, since the pieces of myself seem to have no connection to one another.

Close to my face are dangling catkins. They hang in clusters of three. I break one off and hold the tail-shaped yellow ament in my mitten. Its bracts are like the scales on a turtle's shell. I snap it in two. It's frozen hard, brittle as a candy cane. Inside, it's bright green. *Green!* I break another one. Green again. I look up at the branches. Now they seem catlike, serene with contained knowledge. Spring is harboured in all these buds, a new season packed safely in the catkins, miraculously clinging through wind, sleet, lashing rains.

Across the brook is a massive stand of Joe-Pye-weed. Last summer its head was a furze of purple flowerlets. Now it's a skeleton of brittle, grasping branches; seed-fluff clings to tiny knobs, the knuckles of each flowerlet. The flowers' stalks are hollow as flutes, plunging into the snow. Somewhere beneath the snow the spring green of this plant is curled, waiting.

Everywhere, life is hidden, biding its time, germinating, poised to be quickened by warmth and rain.

The brook water is black as a snake's eyes. I watch its sleek twists, trying to make sense of its formlessness. My eyes travel down and come back upstream, like lures tied to a fishing line.

Down and back, down and back. There's no starting place and no end. It's as disconcerting as looking into the starry sky. I want boundaries. I want to know what is supposed to happen next; yet life becomes more perplexing, less defined. There seem to be no more obvious choices.

A wind stirs the alders. The catkins bounce, then settle back to stillness.

It's a sullen January morning, with leftover snow. A raven flies low and croaks when he sees me. It's a message for others. *Intruder!* There's a trodden look about this place, like a cattle yard. All around my feet, animal trails disappear into the snow at the base of woody-stemmed wildflowers: mice, squirrels, voles, rabbits.

I'm one heartbeat away from lifting my foot and turning for home when something pops out from under a bush. It scuttles across the snow, vanishes as soon as I see it.

Instinct freezes me. Sight is sharpened, hearing quickened, breathing stilled.

It comes out again and runs busily across the snow, nose to ground, weaving rapidly. It's a fat little field mouse, etching patterns in the snow. It scuttles across its familiar territory, dives under the stalks of meadowsweet. It's as ordinary a sight as someone sweeping a floor or breaking eggs into a bowl. It goes about its business, just as the river is going about its business, and the alders with the yellow catkins and the wildflowers with their patient roots are going about their business. I laugh out loud.

Going back over the meadow, tendrils of emotion splinter me. They're delicate as the mouse trail. Just now, striding homewards, I feel as though I'm wrapped in a fragile cloak, its lace the shape of tiny paw-prints.

I duck under the top rung of the barbed-wire fence. I'm heading down another January, the ground rock-hard under my feet and the clouds thinning. I'm clear as the ice and sense the meadow's motion; the planet, turning on its axis, angling ever closer to its star; plants regenerating; the brook running from source to sea; a mouse foraging. *Such wild purity.* I feel an eager yearning I haven't had since childhood.

BLUEBERRY BARRENS AT SUNSET

The mid-winter snows begin. They are different from the fat-flaked snows of December, which brush feathery wings over the earth's skeleton. In late January, storms last for days. Waist-deep drifts obscure doors, bury the garden fence. I walk to the barn with my right shoulder hunched against stinging flakes needling from the northeast. Even though the wood furnace rumbles continuously, it can't keep cold from corners, windows, exterior walls. We close the door of the spare bedroom. Nailheads in the wainscots bristle with frost. Every morning the thermometer reads minus 30 Celsius, and by noon has crept up only a few lines, to minus 24.

We resume work in the studio. Orders at this time of year are scarce. Every year we wonder if people have begun to tire of raku pottery. We create enticing brochures, update our mailing lists, phone galleries, send out the new year's forms. Orders begin to trickle in. *Ten bowls, five medium vases, ten trivets, one covered jar.* In the studio the day's rhythm begins. Slap of clay on the plaster wedging board. Peter with sleeves rolled up, clay dried on his forearms. Hum of the potter's wheel. Sue perched over her table, red-smocked, glasses on her nose, paintbrush clinking the rim of a water-filled Mason jar. CBC radio, the morning show. At the studio desk in the upstairs office, I'm writing orders in the big blue book. Jake's in the last half of his last year of high school. The spruce-clad hills loom behind the snow, suggestive as ships in fog.

I shove back my rolling captain's chair, and the two back casters fall out, as they always do. I stand at the big window. Below me, tails of snow swirl across a shed roof, and I remember how, last November, Peter and I saw winter's genesis. We'd driven to Fundy National Park, parked the car, and hiked down a trail to the lip of a gorge. Far below, a wild river thundered to the sea in waterfall after waterfall. As we slid down a steep hillside, snatching at roots and branches, dank, icy air rose around us. We reached a pool at the base of a cliff. It sucked and slapped the sheer rock face, agitated by tons of water pounding down just above. Long white crystals drifted on the restless water, each icy needle trembling towards the one next to it, as if magnetically attracted. Some touched, coalesced. In minute movements— a quiver, a shift—cold claimed the water and began its work of silencing. On our way home, where there was no evidence, yet, of snow or ice—the tamaracks still golden, cows still at pasture—I knew that winter had begun its work, spinning like a spider in the dark.

Already there are more years behind me than remain to be lived. I put the casters back in the chair legs, sit at the desk, and make my handwriting neat, round, and precise. I take my time over the few orders we have. I feel shut down, suspended, like the insects that travel deep underground, settling beneath roots, leaf mould, and rock crevices, where they assume a stillness that is not quite death; or the mice that make beds of cattail fluff in abandoned birds' nests and sleep the winter away, nose to tail. Leaves packaged within the sealed spiral of buds; snowshoe hares, resting in hollow forms under shrubs, hearts beating inside thick mantles of white fur, paws limp; seeds lying ice-encased in blue light under the tonnage of snow—waiting out the season.

I take a clipboard of orders downstairs. Sue is telling the story of an elderly neighbour who mistook kitty litter for cat food. "Damn cat wouldn't eat!" she imitates his aggrieved voice. "I even put milk on it.'"

Peter and I laugh. He slaps another ball of clay on his wheel. I pause, about to hang the clipboard on a nail. He makes pots like a well-oiled cog in the machine he feels the studio has become. He centres the clay with a few deft pulls and pushes. Every motion is efficient, but his mind is elsewhere. He imagines a broken clay discus—how he might recast some of its pieces in glass or bronze, then put it back together. He sees how its fragmentation makes it a stronger piece.

⁊₂

JANUARY 15, 1995: *I'm feeling time crowding behind me, panicking me. Where is this exact minute that I'm living? Time is an enemy, as real as the bitter wind. What will make me stretch, yawn, unfold in a lovely light?*

Thinking, thinking—a gathering, new self-image. I picture myself in heavy wool socks, jeans, old boots, coming in from the barn. Skis hang on the shed wall. Snow falls from the door frame. I'm stooping to undo my boot laces. I'm a smiley, short, tomboyish woman with many interests, many capabilities. I'm no longer telling myself who I should be. No. I already am, I have become. Within myself is my centre. My job is to be content with this person—to understand my strengths. Not undermine myself by seeking someone, as if who I am is not right here. And underlying all this, a new sense of humour, akin to wisdom.

Lately, I have nightly dreams about Jake. He's always driving away in improbable vehicles, such as milk trucks, and I'm making complicated arrangements to meet him somewhere, afraid that I'll never see him again.

P and I went to the high school talent show. Jake looked great in cowboy boots, black shirt, black jeans. He and Andrew and Wendy performed a song Jake wrote. The restless audience was suddenly intent. Big group of kids around J afterwards. He was like a different person, one we don't see at home—capable, charismatic, not needing a thing from us.

❧

We're surrounded by blueberry barrens, but we can't see them. They're on hills higher than the hills we can see from our house. I forget that horizons shift, that what looms over us might be itself overshadowed. Our hills have a familiar height, defining, for me, the place where earth ends and sky begins. They mark, too, the end of the valley, the limits of my daily world. They're familiar, black against starry skies, flaming orange on October days, cupping our farm like a friendly hand. But when I walk on the barrens, our hills compress, our valley vanishes.

After we've finished work and Jake has arrived home on the school bus, we decide, all three of us, to ski up to the blueberry barrens before supper.

We clip into our skis and sidestep up the enormous snow-bank at the bottom of the driveway where the plow turns. I pull my neck warmer up over my mouth and nose, my eyes tearing with cold. I feel the exhilaration of weightlessness as my knees bend, my legs power, then a long, swift glide. We slide down into the meadow, its snow unbroken by any tracks.

A coyote howls. Jake hears it first, holds up a hand, and we pole to stand still.

It's a long rising note that quavers at its apogee and then holds, stretching the dusk like a tent pole, pulling the dark hills taut; then it drops swiftly to a lower complaint, a progression from demand to query, and the cry quivers until no sound is left.

Smoke rises from chimneys. Our neighbours who work in town—at hardware stores, the ranger station, welding shops—are arriving home. They're making supper, throwing hay to cattle, turning on the TV news. The coyote's cadence scrolls the evening. Anyone walking from barn to house would hear it; yet the call comes from another realm and is as remote, as far from our lives, as are the black-winged ravens who patrol the skies, flying so low that we can hear the pant of their wings.

We wait, but the coyote calls only once again and then falls silent. We push on, skiing fast across the meadow, over the snow-bridged brook, herringboning up the steep field, hoping to reach the top of the barrens in time to see the sunset.

The spice of icy bark rises from spruce trees as we ski for about a mile up an unplowed road, our terrier trotting in our tracks. Abruptly, the forest ends, and snowy expanses spread to the horizon on either side of the road. Empty and rolling as dunes, they're delineated only by the sweeps of shadowed drifts. Rock cairns stand against the reddening sky; beneath a clump of gnarly balsam poplars is a shack, its window boarded shut. Faded paper "Keep Out" signs are tacked to lichened posts. There are piles of uprooted trees silvered by wind and rain; they have a charnel look, like giant bones. Wind rampages unimpeded over the barrens, and the snow is either packed into massive drifts or blown away. Here and there the wiry red branches of blueberry bushes lie naked, exposed, like wind-ravaged islands.

At the top of the barren, Peter and Jake have a sprint. Peter's middle-aged legs move with calm strength, but Jake's have maniacal teenaged energy, and the two modes are equal. They arrive at a cairn at the same instant. I catch up, and we all kick-turn and face the valley, leaning on our poles. We've timed it right: the sun has almost set. It's sliding down behind the western hills, changing from its daytime benevolence to what it truly is—a place of flaming explosion and violence. I squint into the red light, my heart pounding from the long climb. There's one final moment when the sun quivers behind the black trees: long shadows lie blue on the iridescent snow, we feel light on the curves of our cheeks, spruce needles flash. Then the sun settles like sand in a timer and is gone. The air is instantly colder. Shadows are absorbed by darkness, and the snow mirrors the lingering red sky but no longer sparkles.

It is absolutely silent. We stand, surrounded by dark hills, for a long time. Even the dog sits very still, her ears pricked.

Every other year, big tanker trucks grind up the road to burn the fields to make conditions that are perfect for blueberries and difficult for anything else. Afterwards, the hills are black, our boots crunch over charred twigs, we smell oil and smoke, and nothing— spiders, snakes, ants—is left alive. I step my skis around and look to the east and south at the timber company lands: acres and acres of clear-cut, shaved hills that can't be seen from our valley. Snow hides uprooted bushes, mangled roots. Splintered branches are bronzed in the lingering light. I look into the sky, where clouds float like crystal minnows. One star has pricked the blue.

The beauty of the barrens comes not from its ragged contours but from the space left by what is lost. It's like mid-winter itself, when absence grants pre-eminence to constellations, or the voice of wind, or columns of northern lights.

I turn back to watch the day's life drain from the sky.

Peter and Jake push off. They fly down across the snow in their red jackets and wool toques. They seem intensely alive in the luminous evening as they curve down the hill, skis set in the tracks we made coming up.

I wait for a minute, listening to silence, as if, like the coyote's cold and quavering cry, it is itself a language I might one day understand. Its power flows over the poignant lost forests, the empty barrens. I look at the drifting clouds, now burnished coppery red, thinking that it is not this barren land that makes the true context of our valley. These hills are themselves cupped in the black, violent universe. Emptiness is not always desolate, and birth starts in silence. I grasp at an understanding that touches the edge of this thought—but it fleets past and is gone.

I push off and fly down the hill, planning supper, casting my mind over the contents of the pantry.

A BOAT WITH SHIFTING BALLAST

I have the urge to renovate. It's too cold to work on the sauna, although I've been urging Peter to go up there with me.

"Surely there's something we can do."

"No," he says, "wait till March."

Even Kevin raises his shoulders, rubs his hands up and down his freckly arms when I make the suggestion. He shakes his head and talks like Homer Simpson. "Too cold. Hurt fingers. Hammer smash fingers."

The living room is in the southwest corner of the house. It's a perfect winter room, angled away from nor'easters. One window overlooks the lawn, the other frames the valley, and both receive the sun's southerly passage. Years ago we tore out its one interior wall, eliminating a hall and making a curving staircase part of the room. But it's not a cozy place; we haven't yet learned to live in it. Its walls are dirty white, their plaster cracked. A macramé wall hanging holds dusty wildflowers.

There's an oil painting of a runaway lawn mower, made by Peter, hung as a joke and forgotten. It is a room filled with odds and ends of furniture: a misshapen wicker chair with red corduroy cushions; a shag carpet harbouring paper clips and a lost contact lens; pine bookshelves that sag beneath their collection of paperbacks.

Mornings, I work in the pottery studio. Afternoons, instead of going out with my camera or writing, I begin dismantling this room. I reel in Peter and Jake, get them to carry furniture to the back shed. What we can't move becomes a pile in the middle of the floor, draped in plastic. Since the books are arranged by subject and then alphabetically by author—novels, Austin to Woolf; philosophy, Aristotle to Whitehead—I keep them in order by setting them, like dominoes, against the baseboards. They go all the way around the room, twice. I shroud them with sheets. We rip out the shelves.

Peter and I discuss colours. What I want is a peaceful room that will make me wish to stop. Dark blue, we decide—walls, ceilings. Blue with lots of black in it, like a twilit sky. When we bought this house we painted everything white. At twenty-three we wished the walls to recede, as if invisible. We needed space for possibilities. Now I want the walls to bend close and hold me, like a nest. I want to settle rather than fly.

The first roller-load of paint Peter pulls across the white ceiling is so alarming I press my fingers to my mouth.

"Oh my God, it looks like one of those movie theatres in the sixties."

"Just wait," says Peter, with a hint of doubt, drawing another roller-load.

Jake and two friends come into the house. I can hear their boots hitting the floor, then the thud of sock feet.

"What do you think, guys?" I say as they enter the room. Usually, Jake insists on having his opinions heard about any decision to do with the house.

He and his buddies glance. "Nice. Cool."

I'm slightly hurt by his indifference, but he doesn't notice. I see that the boys' eyes are veiled with plans, their off-handed agreement masks impatience. They are always in a hurry, bent towards the next event.

The room is going to be disturbing as long as any white remains. The blue we've chosen is closer to midnight than dusk. I'm worried, but begin work on the walls as Peter finishes the ceiling. As we paint, we listen to music. A clear soprano voice sings a haunting song about how our spirits will endure in the voices of our children. Unexpectedly, tears spring to my eyes, and I wipe them from my cheeks with a painty wrist.

❦

That night the wind rises into a maelstrom. It begins as we yawn about the house, turning off lights, damping the kitchen stove, stoking the wood furnace. Kevin phones. "I just watched a poplar blow over. This is wild. We're going to lose the power." I stand in the living room, cradling my hot-water bottle that I filled from the teakettle. Honeysuckle branches claw the south window. Wind moans in the maples, mutters away, takes another breath, and plucks at the corners of the house. I sense it as something irritable, wanting admittance.

Our small bedroom has a sloped plaster ceiling and is filled by a four-poster bed and a bureau. I settle into my pillows, feet on hot-water bottle, a few books under my bedside lamp. I watch Peter as he stands in the hall wearing only a T-shirt and underwear. He flosses his teeth, methodically, with the same precision with which he inscribes patterns into clay. I hear the clicking of floss, but he's unaware of himself, preoccupied, listening to the wind. He will be concerned with loose roofing, damage to the property, what will happen to his kilns if we lose the power.

Jake's door is shut, but a slice of light steals over the sill and lies sly and soft on the floor. I gaze at it and imagine our son, propped on one elbow, reading. He's too big for his bunk bed. He was in a foul mood when he got home from school. There was nothing I could do to help him, as I might have when he was a child. He was filled with repressed fury, and the expression in his eyes frightened me. After supper the phone rang; a girl asked to speak to him, and he took the portable phone and disappeared into his bedroom. An hour later he emerged, his face smoothed, his lips tight, his eyes tender. We glanced and said nothing. He's determined to find his own answers and resents our attempts to find out what's wrong.

Peter comes to bed. We lie with our backs touching; they feel long and smooth. I remember how, as a child, fear lodged in the small of my back and I needed to stand pressed against a wall until fear faded. There's a snap as Jake turns off his light. The hall falls into darkness. I hear Peter's deep breathing, rising and falling like heavy wings. One by one we drift into oblivion.

I wake from a nightmare.

I snap on the light, slide up against the headboard, and put my hand on my chest; it's slick with sweat. My heart is racing. I look around. There's Peter, steadily breathing as if nothing has happened. I fumble for my glasses on the bedside table. The room resumes around me: a half-sucked lozenge; a mug of water; white door, open onto the hall; the splintery, humped floorboards.

The wind roars in the birch tree just outside the window, flings branches against the porch roof. It moans around the corner of the house and makes a fluttering in the flue. The house is buffeted. I can feel it shake, making the old bedstead shift. The cord hanging from the paper lampshade moves back and forth.

I get out of bed, take my bathrobe from a hook on the closet door, tiptoe into my study, and get my journal and a pen. Going down the stairs, I feel crumbs under my bare feet. I stand in the living room with its raw, sharp smell of paint, its plastic-covered mound of furniture and shrouded books. Its disarray makes the entire house feel unstable, like a boat with shifting ballast.

Cold air eddies around my bare ankles. I go into the kitchen, turn on a light, and curl in the rocking chair next to the stove, where there's a vestige of warmth. I uncap my pen and open my journal. My pen scratches me back towards normalcy. When I'm done writing, I sit for a long time listening to the faint tinkling of wind chimes on the porch.

&

JANUARY 20, 1995: *I had a nightmare about dying. I was walking on a cliff path. Twelve ragged children stumbled behind me. It was a black night and I could hear the ocean. I knew a tidal wave was towering and that, if I continued on the path, I would be swept away, with all the children. I kept on stumbling forward—and woke in a sweat.*

I keep walking on knife-edges. I set myself new tests and perceive that I must either pass or fail. I'm in a constant state of fear. Will I succeed? What will "they" think of me? How will I be judged? The crippling thing for me is this: the feeling that who I am, at my core, will be judged and will fail the test.

I feel stopped. Can't keep trying to capture beauty—with my camera, with words—until I can lose this sense of failure and need of confirmation. Extinction roars in the darkness. It's the tsunami wave. The children are my many selves.

❧

The next morning the temperature has risen dramatically. The house is busy, like a person waiting at a bus stop holding onto scarf, hat, shopping bags. In the fireplaces, ash filters down from the rattling dampers. The stovepipe in the kitchen emits gusty sighs. The door to the boot hall strains at its hinges.

I slide open the sunroom door. It's like coming up over the edge of a sand dune, emerging from heat and quiet into an assault of wind-flung sand and seething combers. The maples and the wind howl, possessing the air, and I feel superfluous, as if I'm witnessing a savage argument.

After breakfast, I put the horses out and watch the chickens pecking their way over the trampled snow to the manure pile with their tail feathers blown up like lady's bustles. The wind carries everything in the same direction. Hay, wisps of timothy grass, loose spruce cones, twigs—everything rushes eastwards on the violent current of air. The white pony's thick, clumped mane sweeps forward as she lowers her neck to eat. Wind-sculpted, it looks like a mane carved in marble.

Peter and I ski out across the fields before going to work. The wind is two-toned. The sound is not coming from anywhere nearby, although the wind presses my coat against my shoulder blades. It comes from way up on the ridge where the clatter of twigs and the crack of branch against branch rise from the tossing maples. But there's a deeper sound too, a steady booming. It seems to be everywhere, this hollow roar—the heart of the day, the core of the storm.

The valley sky is fluid with travelling clouds. They race past in a sublime choreography, purpose integrated with design, like the wishbone of migrating geese.

Suddenly I notice an opening in the clouds.

"Peter! Look up. Right there." I point with my pole. It's only a brief vision, a window onto blue sky. Then cloud veils the opening. It's like the moment when you rest your head on your hands, exhausted from weeping; hope tiptoes up and reminds you that it's always waiting, patiently.

My heart lifts. It is so unexpected—the roiling sky revealing peace.

We stand on our skis at the top of the big field, eyes squinted against the wind, staring down the valley where gusts snatch snow, twist them into spumes, and race them across the fields. I'm thinking of how the naturalist John Muir climbed to the top of a hundred-foot Douglas spruce in the midst of a gale. He chose it carefully, making sure of its "elastic temper." The wild sea of spruces, he felt, were not struggling to survive the danger of the wind but showed "invincible gladness." He clung to his treetop. "With muscles," he wrote, "firm braced, like a bob-o-link on a reed."

On our way back to the studio we take a detour to the sauna bath. Around it, the trees are bending, bowing, but the small building is stalwart; there are no rotten shingles flapping, no loose boards being tugged by the wind. It stands as if waiting. Now that we've turned our minds to it, it's amazing to think of all the years we let it lie fallow, barely remembering its presence.

I tuck a strand of hair under my wool cap. How many times, I wonder, will we go through this renewal? Not so much changing our lives, since we always stay in the same place, as seeing it differently.

Something in me relaxes, lets go—like the spruce cones, torn from their branches, skittering past, riding the wind.

MEN AND WOMEN AT A COUNTRY DANCE

It rains, and then the ground freezes, bare and lumpy. Mercifully, it snows again.

In February there are few orders, and Peter seizes the opportunity to begin work on what he calls his "Fragmentation Series." I work on the living room, and he helps in the evenings. The days are lengthening, and sunset burns in the frost crystals on the storm window just inches away from my nose as I apply paint to the sash.

In my journal is the outline of the book I thought I'd write this winter. It was to be about autumn—about decay, transformation, and the poignancy of process. I would write about the things I love to photograph: brown leaves with purple spines; frost on the blueberry barrens; the fallow soil, furrowed with potatoes. Yet I can neither sit at my desk nor take my camera from its bag. Nothing, it seems, will come to fruition.

᠙

FEBRUARY 5, 1995: *Cleaning the barn this morning, I felt the creeping badness touch me. It's a sense of dread and is connected with the beauty I attempt to capture. Anxiety accompanies wonder. I see a sunset and can only feel sick that I didn't photograph it. Or I fear I will never find the words to describe it. Thus beauty is lost to me, almost as if it does not occur.*

I need to see my creative life as one bubble in a stream: not the central thing that determines whether I succeed or fail, or am worthy, but just one of many bubbles dancing downstream. I wake in the night, lately, with an ache in the back of my throat. There are so many things I'm afraid to let go of: our son; my sense of how my life would be; dreams of things I thought I would do. Time has become finite; for the first time I truly see that it runs out.

Went downhill skiing at Poley Mountain last night. Met Pete W, Judith, Patricia, and Kevin. Nice to be with Patricia and Kevin without the boys, see them as a couple. We skied, wearing face masks beneath goggles. Freezing cold, windy, billows of snow rising from the trees along the trails. Beer in lodge afterwards. Picked up J in town. Talked, amicably, on the way home, about the Nova Scotia College of

Art and Design. He got the application in the mail today—has to pre-pare a portfolio. He's not bothering to apply to any other schools. So, of course, P and I worry.

Cold, cold, today—gently snowing. Minnie lifted her beautiful tail as she pranced out of the barn, and I swept fresh manure out the door after her—warm, pungent smell. Binder twine on the ground frozen in pale loops.

As the heart of our home remains torn apart—littered with paint trays, rollers wrapped in plastic bags, sawdust, plaster-dust, the stepladder, the paint-splattered plastic-covered mound of furniture—I have an obsessive need for order in the rest of the house. My Christmas amaryllis bursts into extravagant bloom. It is as red as a hummingbird's throat, its petals dusted with silver light. I want everything else to be as lovely. Housework takes on new meaning. It imparts calm. I smooth wrinkles from Jake's shirts as I once rubbed his baby back. I ball socks, nest them into the round laundry basket like eggs. I stack sheets, appreciating the simplicity of the task. I can't be in forward motion—something impedes me. I listen to music; women's voices sing to me.

I sleep poorly, with frequent wakings. My subconscious mind is working, even if my creative brain refuses to focus. One night I lie awake, obsessed with how we have made our business into something that is more than either of us, and with how both Peter and I have become dependent on its safety. It provides jobs, money, and busyness. It fills a void. It makes a humming, like a great beehive. It is known, and we are known for it and by it. It has become who we are.

Ten covered jars, twenty-five bowls, six plates, two teapots.

One day I take my finished manuscript from its shelf and read the first sentence: "The coyotes are newcomers." *Boundaries,* I want to call this book. It's about a longing I once had and wrote about. I feel I've betrayed the book, leaving it untouched. My hands are shaking, my heart pounds, but I make phone calls until I have found the number of a publisher in California. I take a long breath and place the call. A pleasant receptionist answers, and I tell her I have a book I would like to show to someone. She connects me to an editor. He's cool, but not dismissive. He asks me about the book, and my voice begins to tremble as I try to describe it. He tells me to send it to him and promises to respond within six weeks.

I hang up and put my hands on the pile of paper, protectively, as if I have misgivings about sending it into the world.

Orders begin to come in, and Peter steps up production. There's so much packing to do that I begin going out to the studio afternoons as well as mornings, instead of working on the living room.

For days the temperature has held at around minus 22 Celsius, the wind making it much colder. Just now the snow is only ankle deep. After lunch, one day, I can't face my dusty packing room without going out into the snowy fields. At the back door, Peter and I kiss each other with our neck warmers pulled over our mouths. I wave a mittened hand and head east.

My camera has taught me that if I set out with an idea of what I'm going to photograph, I'll find nothing. Walking is the same way. If I'm alert, but aimless, I'm more likely to see wondrous things: a robin's egg nestled in a furled leaf; spider babies hatching in a froth of spittle.

The landscape, taken as a whole, doesn't appear to offer much, especially in February. Walking towards the woods, I try to imagine our valley from a city dweller's perspective: white fields, distant hem of green forest, sky, scattered farms, a few pickup trucks on the snow-packed road. The cows are kept inside most of the winter. Imagining a walk, a person would not expect to see much more than trees, sky, and snow. Living in this landscape, I've had to find its particulars—and remember them.

I kick through powder snow, the soil hard beneath my boots. Following the same impulse as the secretive animals, I head for cover, wanting to escape the wind. I jump across the brook, where bent grasses, dragging in the water, are so coated with ice that they've become blunt, white ice fingers. I find myself in a small clearing. The tips of spruce trees whip back and forth against the blue sky. Their branches rise, fall, heavy as supplicating arms, lifting from the trunk, pulling the trees into an anchored waltz. The trees are decorous, like old men and women at a country dance. The sound of wind rises, dies away, then rises again in a soft, rushing roar. It starts as a whispering in needles, but, like backwash absorbed by a greater wave, the sound spirals up until it joins the mighty wind-voice of maples, beeches, tamaracks, alders.

I look at the restless branches and I'm struck by an odd desire. I want to speak. I want to tell them that I, too, exist. It's as if the trees are friends, nodding to one another, speaking their own language, oblivious of my presence.

Then a second feeling surprises me. I feel quietness break and spread within me, like a bud opening. I'm in a place where I can rest from the demands of speech. In the woods, who I am is the same thing as the smell of balsam and bark, as the sound of needles caressed by wind.

The clearing's snow is scrolled with a maze of paw prints. I try to read them but can only guess at whose they are, the way I might ponder a stone megalith, tracing a rune with my fingertip. Hungering for revelation, I see only traces of passage: fresh scat, probably a coyote's; the chain-link claw marks of ruffed grouse; a tail feather. Here are the feathery brush-marks of wings, the hook of a claw, an ochre-yellow piss hole. I leave a trail of my own, a record of wandering absorption.

I'm led into a grove of alders. They're fifteen feet high, flourishing on the banks of the brook, bending a bower of shadow netting over it in summer—a cool place where animals drink. I sit on a fallen alder branch, still springy and thick as my arm. I feel like a rabbit crouched in a thicket, while just across the field is the studio with its telephones, computer, and fax machine; its chattering radio; the hum of Peter's wheel; Sue's lively stories about her twelve brothers and sisters, and how they slept four to a bed—head to toe—milked cows, and chased sheep. And here I sit, listening to the wind, looking at the interlaced twigs against the blue sky. Our neighbour, who is eighty, says the sky isn't as blue as it used to be. But today it's blue as a jay's wing.

Up on the hardwood ridge, a roaring sigh fades and then starts up again. It rushes towards me, tossing the alders when it arrives. The shadows flicker, webbed like a fishnet in shallow water. The wind roves through the spruces, firs, tamaracks. Then it moves on, up over the hill, away. All I can hear is the brook water, plinking beneath ice. The catkins nod, silently, in a remnant of air.

I remember how, as a child, I would listen to the wind and wonder about it. It was close to me, like a friend. Growing up, I grew away.

The wind roams the landscape, tugging, pouncing, chasing snow like a solitary cat. I sense its errant vagrancy. I feel the frozen land, where nothing grows, reaches, speeds, or strives towards any destiny. At the heart of February is not silence but stillness. The quietness that began unfurling in the clearing has spread within me.

Cold settles into my shoulders and my toes. Over my mouth, my neck warmer is stiff as cardboard. I get up, wriggle through the alders, and jump the narrow place in the brook. I stride back across the fields while the wind licks up the snow behind me, erasing my passage.

ONCOMING STORM

The living room is now whole: blue ceiling connects to blue wall. Creamy windows float like clouds on a moonlit sky. The curving birch banister has been stripped of its varnish; its railings are white. This week a friend who is a cabinetmaker installed floor-to-ceiling bookshelves on the fireplace wall. I love the new, thick birchwood that will never sag under the weight of books.

After supper, one night, I sit on the floor leaning against the plastic-draped pile of furniture that still occupies the room's centre.

Upstairs, Jake is memorizing a lengthy Druid incantation. He has been fascinated by ancient history, especially of the British Isles, for his entire life, as if it were his calling. The door of his room is closed, but I can hear his voice rising and falling rhythmically. Peter is sitting at the kitchen table, studying a prospectus for a computer course he wishes to take. His concentration is so complete that it seems to fill the room like a fog that will take time to disperse if I want to speak to him.

I do nothing, neither read nor write in my journal. I feel both stopped and compelled, both frozen and fluid. I'm listening to the house around me. All of us—mother, father, son—have been working so hard: to grow up, make a living, make a family. *It's ending, it's ending.* The words, like Jake's incantation, rise and fall in a remote song whose music is at odds with its words. I feel a realignment inside myself, something that shifts in tiny increments. Tonight I'm thinking about how I took my book to the post office. It was in a manila envelope, with the name of the publishing company written in my firmest handwriting. *Boundaries,* a lovely thing, separate from me—gone, now. And, suddenly, I want never to write again, never to take another photograph. I want to stop striving, caring, endeavouring to make something that is mine, *me,* my voice, and hating myself for failing. I sit on the living-room floor, staring at a new vision of myself as though it lies inches away from my nose, a frozen form.

Later, I call one of my closest friends. Her marriage is faltering. There are long silences as she struggles to speak through tears.

Long after Peter's deep, rough breathing changes to the soft, nearly silent breath of deepest sleep, I lie awake. At one in the morning, I go downstairs, barefoot, and stand in the sunroom, looking at the stars. There's no moon, and the sky is a lustrous slate-black. All the way to the horizon the stars glitter, making a dome of jewelled splendour as encompassing as the blue bowl of a summer's day. I pull open the glass door and step outside, hugging my long flannel nightgown tight against my body. The stars are gold, blue, smoky red, silver, green.

I hear the muted mutter of water running beneath ice. The barns and the maples are black silhouettes. The dark land lies like an afterthought while the night sky wheels past, or, rather, we wheel through it, travellers in a galaxy. How strange, I think, that we sleep beneath this spectacle—that we pull quilts over our heads and seek oblivion.

I awake the next morning from a restless sleep. It's pitch dark, and downstairs the dog scratches her fleas.

My grandparents once slept in this bed. My grandfather lay on Peter's side, and my grandmother on mine. Their plaster ceiling, like ours, sloped low over the bed. On Sundays, when my family went to their house for dinner, I went upstairs with my girl cousins. Our patent leather shoes tapped against the wood floor of their spartan bedroom. We looked at ourselves in the tarnished mirror. If I spent the night, I watched my granny take pins from her bun, brush her long grey hair, and plait it into a braid. My grandfather, big-bellied, sat on this very bed, his blue-veined white feet shedding their slippers. I'm lying on my side, imagining this scene so vividly that I can smell their house: wool, old furniture, gas leaking from the stove, apples; I hear their voices—his rumbly, hers whispery—and see their placid, kindly faces. I'm shocked at the span of years that has come flooding between that moment and this one.

We stumble into another day. I let in the cats, Peter stokes the furnace. Jake takes a lengthy shower. A band of red over the forest is quickly absorbed by clouds. Then there's a hopeless light that makes the worst of the pumpkin pulp from last Hallowe'en's jack-o-lanterns squashed on the brown grass, exposed by a recent rain. Chickadees chatter in the ragged rose bush. The radio announces a winter storm warning: 90- to 100-kilometre winds, 40 centimetres of snow.

I go out with Jake. We walk down the drive to the point where it joins the lane. Once he was my little boy, holding my hand, leaning against my leg, asking questions. Once I knelt with my arm around him, pointing at the sky. "Who has seen the wind, neither you nor I, but when the trees bow down their heads, the wind is passing by!"

He's taller than I am. He's passed the stage when he patted me on the head, exclaiming, "You are so little!" Now he's used to my smallness. One day I took him by the shoulders and realized he was stronger than I was. We've scrapped like brother and sister, yelling, slamming doors in each other's faces. We're now at a new stage. He's developing tolerance towards me, a wary friendliness, as if he's beginning to see me as a separate person whose embarrassing peculiarities he may be able to change. We see each other's faults, but we also begin to appreciate the things about each other that make us similar. He loves to tell me his dreams and to listen to mine. We like to analyze people—his friends, our friends, and especially the girls he's no longer going out with. We faithfully watch a few TV shows together. He complains to me about Peter. I try to give him perspective on his father's reasons and needs.

We cross the bridge halfway down the lane.

"Aaron has this amazing guitar. We're getting together tonight, him and me and Corey. We'll have a keyboard, drums, penny-whistle. Corey can sing really well."

"No. *Corey?* I can't believe it. *He* and *I*," I add.

I love knowing his friends. It makes me feel young, as if I'm their age. Or maybe I make them feel like adults. I realize, as we reach the end of the driveway, that just as we begin to be equals, they will all go away.

At the end of the lane, he stops.

"Bye, Mum."

He heads down towards the spot where Amy and Alyson are waiting for the bus. Long legs, backpack slung on one shoulder. As soon as he leaves me, one shoulder slouches and his eyes become hard. The cowboy walk of seventeen.

I turn back. The air has warmed just enough to smell the iron scent of snow. The land lies entirely open, exposed. I walk down to the pond, stand on its banks, and look out over this end of the valley: the meadow with its red alders marking the meandering river; the feathery grasses tugged by an uneasy, fore-running wind. A feeling comes from the land itself. It's like coming upon a hibernating animal and seeing the secret of endurance: catkins are tightly sheathed; buds are buried deep. Like a bear, the earth remains asleep while the winds rage and the snow drives upon it. Every creature has its own sources of sustenance.

A thin plume of smoke wavers from the chimney of our white clapboard farmhouse. Like the land, the house seems braced, shut up tight, the storm windows putting double glass against the cold, the foundation banked with fir boughs, the storm door swung shut.

In that house we'll grow old. I sense a new task before me: how to sustain myself. Time is like an oncoming storm.

ICE SPIDER

The predicted snow came as slicing rain. Then there was a cold snap. Now the soil is frozen so hard it's like walking on pavement. I feed the horses and stand in the back door of the barn. The sun has set behind the hardwood ridge. The honeysuckle bush is a black frieze against the red sky, and I see a nest wedged in a fork of its branches. I didn't notice it last summer, hidden in the pink flowers. The bush stirs on the evening's breath, and the nest, riding the motion, interrupts the sequence of trunk, branch, and twig with its homey presence. I walk to the bush and stand on tiptoe to peer in. The inner layer is a tweed of black and white horse hair, the outer layer a frail shell of straw-pale grasses twisted round and round, woven, their ends tucked one under the next. If I held it, it would fill the palm of my hand like an egg. I could add it to my collection of bones and antlers, but I hesitate, wondering if the birds are planning to use it again.

Darkness creeps from the hedgerows, carrying the cold. On the hills the trees are flushed by the setting sun, giving the illusion of warmth. A single star makes the sky indeterminate; it's not yet a night sky, but neither is it day. One thing is in the process of claiming another; the minute I'm living is, at the same instant, the minute I'm remembering. I stand gazing at the new star and feel the folding of time.

Peter and Jake are in the house visiting with Kevin, who stopped in after work. He's having a beer with Peter, and then Jake's going up to their house to babysit the four boys. The boys love Jake. He tells them stories so terrifying that, sometimes, he tells me, he even scares himself.

There's a casserole in the oven. I glance at my watch: half an hour until it's done, so I take a quick walk up over the frozen field. I stride up the hill, cross a field, and come down a slight slope to the brook that twists from the edge of the woods. Last week the river overflowed its banks and completely submerged the plank bridge. Now the water lies in frozen slabs and swirls, green, softened by the flush of sunset, slashed with black shadow. I drop to my hands and knees and crawl onto the slippery bridge. A spruce branch is imbedded in the ice. It must have been underwater, tugging and bouncing in the water; now it's frozen solid. Wispy grasses, too, were captured; they poke through, each stem encased in a funnel that curves away out of sight, like a glass straw. Drifts of blue bubbles are suspended just beneath the ice's surface—galaxies floating within white shards. There are jagged fractures, crystal spears.

I'm creeping along, exploring this universe with my nose almost touching the ice, fascinated by the frozen world, when I start and take a sudden breath. *Spider!* A small brown spider with a black cross on its back. It's frozen solid. Two of its legs are encased in ice funnels; its body, and its other legs, are free. In all this expanse of frozen, rain-swept countryside, this is the only creature I've seen. There are no birds, no animal tracks, no sound but rattling branches. I lie on my belly, chin in hand. The warm, earth-smelling air of last week's thaw awakened this spider and lured it out. I imagine the grip of ice on its legs, its futile grasping.

My thighs begin to freeze, so I stand up carefully and back away. Even when I'm on the other side of the bridge, I look back and can see the black spot, like a drop of blood on white linen.

Walking back, my face freezing as the sun truly vanishes, I remember last summer, when pink rhodhora blossoms, there by the brook, were linked by necklaces of dewed spider silk.

CLOUDS AND MOUSE TRAIL

Sometimes the two worlds we inhabit—the world of the studio, the world outside the windows—become so distinct that I can hardly believe in the one I'm not currently in. It's like reading about heat in the dead of winter and not being able to imagine it.

I sit at my desk, talking to a shipping company in Montreal. The woman asks me how many cartons I'm shipping, their weight, value, destination. English is not her first language; neither is French. I wonder about her life, this person who spends her days typing such information onto a computer screen. Does she wonder about me? For my part, I'm surrounded with the boxes of pottery I've packed, along with a confusion of shredded paper, invoice books, and packing tape. The phone rings, but it's the other line, and no one can answer it because I've been put on hold, and Peter is firing.

My packing room becomes extremely hot: in the next room, Peter opens the kilns. The wall fan springs to life, trash can covers clank, and there's a creaking of the counterbalanced chain that lifts the kiln lids. Red-hot pots sizzle and hiss in water. There's a mix of smells: the antiseptic dryness of hot clay; the green-wood smoke of burning sawdust.

I put down the phone and organize my papers in a small ritual that puts a stop to this part of my life. All afternoon I've hardly glanced out the window. I've been listening to the radio, taping bubble wrap around pots, breathing paper dust, heaving boxes onto scales, thinking about other things I could have done with my life, worrying about Jake or my parents, racing up to the office to rip a fax off the machine, talking on the phone about a studio tour for the Corn Hill Women's Institute.

I put on my coat, neck warmer, toque, mittens, and cross-country ski boots. I push open the studio door and step out onto the deck, where my skis are propped in the snow.

I pause between the two worlds, glancing at my watch. It's five o'clock: Jake will have returned on the school bus, and

I should go make supper. Still, it's blue twilight, the snow is flushed by the setting sun, and my ears are shocked by the utter absence of sound.

This sensation is familiar. I am irresolute, feeling two different kinds of responsibility, two conflicting desires. Both seem equally evanescent: the winter's dusk and the passage of family.

As I stand considering, the silence claims me. It's as if someone has laid firm hands on my shoulders and turned me towards the fields. I clatter my skis onto the snow, snap my boots into the bindings, work mittened hands into pole loops. The horse and pony, waiting at the barn door, throw up their heads, startled, and then watch with mild curiosity as I begin the long ski up the hill. The breath from their nostrils makes white plumes in the darkening air.

Below me, our place is so much like the toy village from Germany I had as a child that I can remember the feel of the wooden church in the tips of my fingers. I can remember easing the houses into place by holding their chimneys, delicately, and placing cotton wool against them, for snow.

I stand still for a long time, like the horses, until I'm part of this world, and the other one fades like a dream.

Shoals of cloud curve like wave-ribbed sand across the evening sky. Pearl-grey, nacreous as a shell's lining, they are flushed silver-pink. Down at the end of the valley, the volcanic sky smoulders in layers of red, orange, and molten yellow, and the hills are black. I can see individual spruce trees on the western ridge, sharp as lace.

The snow is flocked with thousands of scallop-shaped drifts. Each holds an edge of blue light. I notice tiny mouse prints. The line made by the tail, delicate as a grass-stem, connects the linked paw prints. It is the tiniest trail I've seen this winter, a thread curving across the field. I follow it; where the mouse jumps, there's a sixteen-inch gap, and then the trail stitches away again, as far as I can see. Each tiny print holds a chip of blue shadow. I stop, not wanting my footprints to mar this loveliness.

It is so simple and so perfect. The tiny creatures of the earth sculpt with their feet, leave evidence of their presence, frail as the brush of wind on water.

I look up at the sky. The clouds, drifting in a long, sinuous funnel, mirror the passage of the mouse across the snow-covered field. I'm looking from one of the smallest details on the planet up into the vastness of space. And the two things are connected, as if this bowl of sky were close and familiar; as if the clouds had witnessed the animal's passage.

A TUFT OF WHITE FUR

It's no longer dark when Jake leaves to catch the school bus. The kitchen is filled with young light. Outside, on the honeysuckle by the east window, snow-crystals spin fluffy bridges from twig to twig. Occasionally, one collapses, leaving a shattered rainbow.

Jake opens the door to the boot hall, and icy air slices into the kitchen. He looks at me as I sit at the table, elbows among crumbs and marmalade. He's wearing army boots, an Irish tweed cap, and a heavy wool coat. He hesitates, a question in his eyes. "Bye, Mum," he says. I see him considering his needs, his obligations. So I make myself smile. "Bye, hon." He shuts the door, gently.

I stare at the seed catalogue propped against a teapot. To plan a garden, like planning a life, means that you can imagine something larger than the individual parts. You see how one thing flows into the next. I pull the catalogue towards me and turn the shiny pages. My mind registers names—*Rossa di trento lettuce, Giant Musselburgh leek, Alaska hybrid cantaloupe, Royal Chantenay carrot*—but I don't visualize seedlings breaking through loam on a summer's morning. I don't imagine a wheelbarrow filled with carrots or the taste of a sun-warmed tomato. All I can see is the effort of detail.

Evening grosbeaks and blue jays make a tremendous flurry at the feeder just beyond the window, but their squabbling cries are dim, like echoes of whatever it is I've lost.

Peter comes running downstairs. His mind is always on his list of what needs to be done. He wears tension like a backpack. Our moods are like colliding ball bearings. They crash together and send each other in opposite directions. He pauses at the door. I raise one hand in a desultory wave. "I'll be out soon," I say. He looks at me just as Jake did, worried, beseeching.

I pour tea and watch the steam swirl in the sunlight.

੭৶

FEBRUARY 15, 1995: *A dream: I had a flowerpot full of black mud and I was trying to stick some lovely, fragile white flowers upright in it, but they kept disappearing, getting drowned, broken, submerged.*

A feeling, lately, of nothing holding any promise or potential. A sense of life being over. What do I really care about? Where do I want to put my energy?

Does the coyote, I wonder, care what it has or has not done? Do the partridge, scratching their nightly nests in the snow, worry about whether they will survive the night? What does the snowshoe hare ponder as she hides from the fox? How do I live my own winter, like the unclad animals? Like them, I've closed down. My leaves have fallen. My flowers are fading, their petals dropping, one by one.

Jake's cat has cancer of the mouth. We could send him to Charlottetown and have his tongue removed. Instead, we wait for the day when it's clear to us that his suffering is so bad that we must have him put down.

He's a big yellow tom, inappropriately named Sweetie. He goes for walks with us, like a dog, trotting through the woods on soundless paws. When Jake was a child and lay on his belly drawing swords and dragons, Sweetie curled on the floor beside him, eyes half-shut with pleasure, rapturously kneading Jake's sweater.

At lunch, today, Sweetie paces into the pantry where his food is kept. A strand of drool sways from his mouth. He can't eat dry food anymore. I open a can of sardines. He stands on his back feet, paws on my leg. He loves fish so ardently we have to put him outside whenever we have it in the house, or he becomes demented, cross-eyed with craving. I drop to my knees, stroking him as he attacks the fish. It falls from his mouth, and he makes a great anguished yowl.

I phone the vet. *Today, please. After Jake gets home from school. Thank you.*

꙰

Late that afternoon I make sure Sweetie's in the house, and then I go up into the woods. A cloud withdraws from the sun and the snow suddenly glistens; shadows stripe the snow in blue lines, like another forest. I cup my mittened hand on a maple, feeling its ribbed bark, notice a colony of winter mushrooms on a fallen birch; their tiny lily-pad heads have all reoriented themselves to drop their spores earthwards. Golden beech leaves lie on the snow like paper boats, filled with snow crystals.

I hear the brook. There's no other sound in the woods—no rush of wind, no creak of branch or patter of twigs, no birdsong— only the purling of water.

I go down towards the brook. In spring I'd be wading through beds of Dutchman's breeches, furled ferns, white violets. Now I'm in a cathedral of trees where every bough, branch, and twig is outlined in snow, and the dark tracery lies motionless against a background of white, as if a secret tapestry has been revealed.

I squat by the brook, listening to its cable of sound. There's no nuance. It is not saying one thing and meaning another. It's a sound without emotion, yet it has authority. It makes me pay attention.

Snow shakes loose from the trees, then stretches into shimmering sheets that drift and slowly fall.

I try to imagine a life without purpose. I try to imagine a life where one moment is connected to the next like the droplets of this river.

On the way to the vet's, Sweetie raises himself from Jake's arms and cries, just once. Jake and I say nothing all the way to town.

I write a cheque at the desk. We wait. Fish swim in a tank, but Sweetie pays no attention. He breathes in short pants, his mouth open. His eyes are black. I put my head down to look into them, but see only the inward stare of pain. I want him to recognize my compassion. "Mum," Jake whispers. He is stern. We carry the cat into the operating room. The woman vet looks one last time at his tongue and shakes her head. They shave a tiny patch on the cat's leg.

"It's all right, it's all right," I say, stroking his head, wanting him to hear my voice. The needle enters. He draws away, startled. Then his body settles.

I turn and bury my face in Jake's shoulder.

We ski up to the top of the hill. The cat's eyes are half-open. Jake poles with one hand, holds Sweetie in the crook of his arm.

We can't bury him, but we arrange his body on the snow, tucking his nose between his white paws. We cut branches of spruce, curving layers like feathers, branch over branch, until we can't see his tiger-striped fur. Then we take stones from an old cairn, hard rock in mittened hands, and pile them over the branches, rock on rock.

I put my arm around Jake's waist, and he puts his arm over my shoulder. Through a chink in the cairn, I see a tuft of white fur. Jake left a crack, a window, so Sweetie could see the sky.

Fur to bone to earth.

The sun is setting, and around the cairn the snow breaks the fire into fragments. We put on our skis, lean to snap the bindings, work mittens through the pole loops. I look up at Jake before we push off. He's looking down the valley to the place where the hills pleat into blue folds. His eyes are not bewildered or hurt. They're not child's eyes. They are mute, patient. They stare into pathways of oncoming sorrow, as if he realizes that this loss is a beginning. I wonder if he's beginning to shield his heart.

We stand together, listening to emptiness. There are no answers to the questions we would ask, if there were someone to ask, someone to hear.

SPRING

WREATH BURNING

It's the first day of spring, a Saturday. Jake spent the night at a friend's house, and Peter and I have just come yawning into the sunroom. Every year we haul a rickety shelf unit into the glass-doored sunroom off the kitchen to start our seeds. Even though the fields are still covered in snow, this room smells of moist soil. Wavering lines of green shoots push against the plastic wrap snugged over the seedlings: tomatoes, broccoli, cabbage, zinnia, and calendula. I tend them like orphaned kittens, tipping the narrow nozzle of my watering can and letting sun-warmed water seep into the soil, drop by drop.

Over toast and coffee, we make a list of things we'll need for the sauna bath.

> 2" x 3" spruce
> 4" x 8" milled beams
> vermiculite
> plastic
> nails
> lag bolts
> beer, cocoa, marshmallows

Tomorrow, Kevin, Patricia, and the boys will spend the day with us, and we'll begin building.

After breakfast, Peter and I go out on our snowshoes. The snow is knee deep, with corn snow on top. It's wet, fast, perfect for skiing, but before heading for the hills we're going to haul two massive timbers up to the sauna. After our first pottery studio burned over twenty years ago, we dismantled the old cow barn for its hand-adzed beams. We used most of them to build a new studio, but a few were left over and have been in the barn ever since. We manoeuvre them onto our longest wooden toboggan and lash them in place. Peter and I lean into the manila rope. The rope cuts across my stomach, and I watch the varnished wood of my snowshoes lift and fall, a waffle of snow pressing up through their webbing. The beams begin to slide, and we stumble forward. We crunch across the pasture, heading for the woods. The horse and pony lift their heads from their hay and prick their ears. Two ravens change course and cruise over us. Peter caws at them; they veer abruptly with alarmed *quorks* and vanish over the hill.

The sun is intense, reflecting off the snow and onto our faces. Everything seems tenuous, infirm. The snow crystals expand. Springtail insects, or snow fleas, appear like pepper, the first sign of spring. Ten million per acre, they come swimming up through the snow, propelled by two legs on the last segment of their bodies. The legs unclasp, and the tiny black dots teem and percolate. A minute spider crawls across the snow, and a winged bug. Chickadees have begun their spring mating song: *swee-tee, swee-tee.*

We stop, panting. "I was thinking," I say.

There's something I've been wanting to say, but haven't dared, which surprises me about myself. It's awkward, shaping a new intention with words. "I was thinking of using the upstairs part of the sauna bath as a writing cabin."

Peter trudges on without saying anything. There's a beat, like a silent measure in music when the last note resonates. Snow grinds beneath our snowshoes. The air smells of spruce trees. The blue sky seems large, inviting. I feel that the form of our life is shifting.

"You could put a little wood stove up there," he says. He can't help himself. He's examined the idea, sensed its implications, and immediately begins to see an actual place. Whereas for me, it's still only a feeling, like the warmth flushing my cheeks.

We lean into the rope again, grunting. My heart hammers. I love feeling rugged, working next to Peter. Hips, calves, shoulders, wrists—I'll ache tonight. Sunburned, I'll drift into sleep drugged on the wine of March wind.

We haul the timbers as close to the sauna bath as we can get. We unlash them from the toboggan, kneel in the wet snow to roll them off. Then we stand, brushing snow from ourselves. The sauna looks stripped, like a room ready to be painted. Anything half-connected or rotten—window, porch, doors, floor—was removed last fall. Already, it appears less derelict.

We stand for a while, sketching the air with our hands.

"Let's put a little window in the door of the bath," Peter suggests. "And a good set of stairs."

"With a twisty tamarack railing."

❧

We go to town later, get supplies, and pick Jake up from school. When we get home, patches of dirt are appearing in the snow-packed driveway, exuding cold dampness. In the kitchen window, against a reflection of hills, there's a blur of blue wings as jays fight over sunflower seeds in the feeder. The afternoon scatters into tail-ends as Jake hauls his schoolbooks and backpack into the house, as Peter begins unloading lumber and beer, as I carry in bags of groceries.

Spring is jostling me. I'm not ready to let go of winter, the frozen world within which I, too, felt suspended. Jake's calling to me, and I'm telling him where I put his penny-whistle, I'm easing down a bag of groceries on the kitchen table and noticing how the western light picks out crumbs on the floor, dust on the wood stove, and I'm thinking: *I need an equinox ritual.*

I let the thought float until it snags on the Christmas wreaths. There they are, still hanging, red ribbons faded, forlorn as the sauna.

After putting away the groceries, I pocket a pair of wire clippers, then gather kindling, newspapers, and strike-anywhere matches. I go back outside, loop the wreaths over my arm, and head for the vegetable garden.

The snow is deep in the garden: it's mounded in the raspberry canes, caught by the sweet-pea trellis and the pea fence, drifted on the manure pile, and blown against the skeletal 'Mammoth Russian' sunflowers. As I stomp into it, made cumbersome by wreaths, a shovel, and fire-makings, snow slithers over the tops of my boots, wets my socks, freezes my feet. I dig a pit in the snow, crumple paper, make a tent of kindling. Then I begin snipping the wire that lashes the boughs to their masonite backing. I lay a few boughs in the pit, strike a match on the zipper of my jeans, cup it in my hand, and touch it to the pyre. Flame steals quietly into the cave of paper, then bursts crackling in the fir. The needles ignite separately, in a flash. Smoke wavers up in a thin, blue coil, and straightens as the wind catches it. I peel the boughs from the wreath and drop them onto the fire. It crackles with a sound like dry sticks being trampled by a multitude of tiny feet.

Bough after bough bursts into flames, become red ladders that flare, pulse, and fade to grey. Finally, every one is gone, and I stand poking the ashes, aware of how the evening clouds are streaking the sky over the eastern hills, and the shingled buildings, spring-damp, are darker. I shove the faded ribbons into my pockets. Nothing is left except next year's round wooden rings. Under the black twigs and feathery ashes, the snow has melted.

It's the first time I've ever set fire to something I once loved.

৯৹

MARCH 22, 1995: *Tonight I stood in my study over the kitchen. There's an Ansel Adams print on the wall; coyote skulls, gull feathers, piles of books. I looked at my desk and work table, more or less abandoned since early January: notebooks, mattboard, computer. For the first time in weeks I felt excited about making new slides, about returning to my book about harvest. I thought what a relief it would be to have a clear sense of direction and purpose. I need to figure out my relationship to the pottery studio. I need to stand behind myself, to support my own talent and capabilities. I need to know who I am and what I do and state it clearly, to feel part of an ongoing process rather than inhibited and trapped by the past. I want this to happen. I want to be calm, yet filled with energy.*

At the health food store I talked to S about kids leaving home. One of hers is gone, the other leaving next year. Her eyes filled with tears. Her hands shook as she poured oatmeal into a paper bag. We were pregnant together. I can't get used to the fact that all of this is now part of the past: pregnancy, babies, kindergarten, school. Kids make time so apparent. Will there be more space, more time, when we no longer watch our children grow?

P went to hospital for another stress test. Something is not right for him either. His back hurts, his hands ache. He's not excited about making pots anymore, even though he is so good at it. Odd. We have what we've always wanted—a thriving studio, the orders, the income. But we've let the studio overhead, of both money and stress, get too high. Maybe we've just been doing this for too long. P seems frustrated, just as I am.

BOYS AND WET MITTENS

Patricia makes a chair for her youngest son. She puts a cinder block as close to the bonfire as possible and sticks snowshoes into the snow behind it for a back. She piles a few logs in front of the chair for Zane's soaked feet. No one else pays any attention to his woeful face, his tears. She kneels and rubs his chapped feet.

"There you go!" I hear the cadence of repair, like a musical motif: three strong soothing notes. She puts her own mittens on his bare feet. He looks like a cheerful orangutan with his round, brown eyes, his rubbery smile.

All around the bonfire are salvaged boards, pushed into the snow like a primitive fence. They're steaming, as are the wool mittens propped around the fire on sticks: red, blue, striped. Zane works a marshmallow onto a long alder branch. The three older boys are making a bridge across the river. Jake is up on the scaffolding with Kevin and Peter.

"Hey," Kevin yells. Everyone looks. The boys have dislodged a bottle of beer from an icy pool. It's bobbing downstream. They race after it, making ineffectual stabs with ski poles.

Patricia and I are occupied with tidying while the men build. It occurs to me that our activity might be construed as keeping house while they go to work, but it's what we want to do. We clear up dead fir trees that have fallen nearby, casualties of a bud-worm epidemic. We hook our hands in the forks of branches, brace our feet, and tug. The trees slide towards the fire. Flex, pull of muscle. Our leather outer-mitts are soaked black. The fire makes a steady crackling gobble, searing white-hot at its heart. The wind shifts, sends smoke into our faces, then spreads it down the brook. Snowshoes and skis lean, criss-crossed, in the snow. There's an intermittent whine of battery-powered saws and spurts of sawdust. Chunks of lumber fall and fly from Peter's and Kevin's and Jake's saws. The men are replacing the floor-joists of the second storey. Bit by bit, a strong, yellow grid appears. I watch their masculine rhythm, with its mixture of self-absorption and banter, application and pause. Their hammers ring and ring, then clang into holders at their waists as they call down, "Hey! Somebody send up a timber." One of the boys runs up, squats, slides up a square-sided plank.

"Come on, guys," Patricia calls to her sons. Hauling empty toboggans, we head down to the barn for another load of supplies.

Snowy fields spread around us as we leave the edge of the woods. I'm sliding forward on skis, a toboggan swishing behind me, so hot from exertion that I've stuffed my toque in a pocket. My hair smells of woodsmoke, and my hands are sweating inside my mittens. As I leave the trees and glide into the field, the space between snow-glitter and blue sky makes me feel small, weightless, as if I might lift from the ground. The snow is watery beneath the noonday sun, and there's the smell of oranges as Nick, the second youngest, stumbles past me on snowshoes, peeling one. We move away from one another and become smaller in scale, like people at the beach.

Down at the barn we stack spruce boards on the toboggans: clatter of wood on wood. We heave a heavy box of spiral nails, a paper bag of screws, bungee it all in place, and head back up over the fields.

"Look at that," I say to Patricia. "There's a pinkness in the trees."

She stops, pleased. "So beautiful, isn't it?" She's a prairie girl, still amazed by hills.

"How can it be? Another winter, gone." And I wonder, glancing at her, so much younger than I am, if she thinks I'm like an old lady, constantly wringing time from a sponge. Time seems to condense and settle, like the snow. Perhaps, eventually, it ceases altogether.

As we near the clearing by the brook, we see that the men have come down from the scaffold and are lifting the lids of cast-iron pots with long sticks. The smell of chili and potatoes rises with the wet-wool steam. We park the toboggans by the sauna and squat by the fire, scrabbling in cardboard boxes, digging out enamelware bowls, spoons, mugs. The sauna bath wears its new lumber, bright as a promise that I make to myself.

TWO TREES

MARCH 28, 1995: *Friday night. Jake is spending the weekend with Corey. Hope they'll be sensible, but there's nothing we can do about it anymore. In a way it will be easier when he's in Halifax, because then I won't even know when to be worried. Patricia and Kevin have taken the boys to a ski area in Maine. Pete W and Judith are in Mexico for six weeks, as are quite a few other friends. P and I have two days entirely alone. We didn't make any plans.*

Today it was cloudy—no sunlight to glitter in the patches of snow or tip shadows into hollows. Spruce trees crouch at the edge of the brown fields like disconsolate bears. It's been warm, rainy. The patchy snow is unskiable.

I feel odd tonight in our big, quiet house. P went back to the studio. I realize I need to find something out of place I should fix—a small project like cleaning a bedroom—but I can think of nothing that inspires me to action. Friends seem distant: I feel no pressure to address anyone else's needs. I wonder if this is what it will be like next year. P and I are lonely, although we don't say it to each other. It's a raw feeling, unveiling our couplehood, making us sense an intimacy that we've had no time for lately or have been avoiding. Being alone on a weekend is a bit like staying in a vacation cottage. There's an element of ritual, rather than necessity, to much of what we do. Space surrounds us. We return to ourselves, gather up our scattered threads, and begin to reweave them. There's less, and there's more. I can make choices, rather than respond to situations. In the childless house I become aware of things I've never said, but now articulate; and things I've never thought of before, but don't. I talked about this with Patricia recently. She can't imagine living alone with Kevin, since they've had boys for so long. We both wonder if we'd stay here in the valley if our husbands died. She's given this some thought, since Kevin works at such a dangerous job—underground in the potash mine. She says she'd stay. I wonder if I could bear to live in this big house alone. I wonder if other women, or men for that matter, trickle this thought through their minds. Being part of a couple, like anything, bears its price of vulnerability.

On Saturday, in the early afternoon, the wind begins to mutter. It sweeps up from the sea like a flume channelled by steep hills, until it breaks against windows, porches, gutters, steel roofing, lilac bushes—the outcropping where we live. It rises in force and insistence, whistling, moaning, until we are made aware of the silent still-life of the house's interior: dried hydrangeas on the piano, dusty geranium leaves. Infected, seduced, we put on our coats and boots, pick up our walking sticks in the hall, and step out the back door.

Instantly, we're not in charge anymore. The dog's ears are blown inside-out. A stick comes scuttering down the driveway.

We come to a quick agreement about which way to go. I can't trace the precise path of communication. After twenty-six years of marriage, we've lost the energy to argue about small decisions.

We set out across the pasture, jumping from tuft to tuft in the marsh, hurling ourselves across the brook with the help of our walking sticks, ducking the barbed wire by the oak trees that we planted from seed, striding across the upland hayfield where the ground is firm and I can smell earth and mud. We walk up a steep trail, a lane of compacted snow down its centre left by a winter's skiing. On either side, clumps of reindeer moss have appeared, glinting with water drops; my boots slip on wet leaves. The spruce trees bow and bounce, their tips lashing.

When we reach the hardwood ridge, the wind's roar augments; it dives and twists in the brittle twigs. The path heaves, actually rising and falling beneath our feet, rocked by the peaty soil humping up as trees see-saw against their roots. I put my arms around a young maple, crane my head to watch its topmost branches flinging forward, whipping back, and I feel the subtle, lithe swaying of the tree until I'm slightly dizzy, as if I'm standing on the deck of a ship—just for an instant my body knows that the earth beneath me is not really hard but is as fluid, as wildly alive, as sky or sea.

The trail is so high over the valley that, as we look down on church, barns, and fields, the space between them compresses and the place seems foreign. We walk in the wind-lashed woods. The air smells of thawing moss and ice. We see lichens, deer prints, squirrel middens. Peter calls, beckons. We always need to share our discoveries. Once he waited for me to catch up, just to show me the place—there was nothing left to see—where a partridge had burst from its hiding place under the snow and exploded into his face. *This is where it happened!* he told me, jabbing his ski pole into the snow, making me a witness, if to nothing tangible, then at least to his wonder.

This time he has discovered two trees: a maple and a spruce. Their trunks lie across each other at precisely the angle at which my hands, laid before me on a table, make an angled cross. The trees have been grinding against each other for so long, tossed by the same winds, sharing the same weather, swaying in rhythm, that, where they touch, each tree has planed the other one flat. All peculiarities have been worn away; the flesh is as yellow and raw as fresh lumber. Heartwood is exposed, and growth rings; sawdust has been trickling down the trunks so steadily that a cobwebby fungus has spawned.

I come up the trail to marvel at this. I put my hand on the maple, not looking at Peter, absorbed in my own perception of his discovery. In this place of random interruptions, of sudden stops and slow starts, of curves and runnels, it's unusual to see such a mechanical pattern, deliberate as the strokes of a waterpowered saw blade. I put my ear to the bark to see if I can hear anything, and I fancy I can. It's collusion as well as collision; they accommodate each other, but not without sacrifice. They'll grow closer and closer, but inevitably one will die, leaving the other with a strange scar that will become smooth, as it heals, so that no one who had not seen this sight would know what had caused it.

❧

And then we awaken, on Sunday, to a hushed, foggy day. I can't see where the hills stop and the sky begins. The hardwood trees fade away, ghosting into the gloom until only the dark spruce trees prick through; and, as the white mists drift across the hillsides, even those sharp spires vanish, appear, and vanish again. The landscape is different every time I look out the window.

Peter decides to work in the studio much of the day, even though it's Sunday. He's obsessed with a rubber-mould technique that allows him to cast bones, skulls, and twigs in bronze. So I decide to clean house. I put music on the stereo and I dust, vacuum, polish. If I could be in two places at once, I might hover outside in the mist and hear a faint cacophony: drums, saxophone, the thrumming of a vacuum cleaner. I spend the day listening to electronic voices. They are real people, singing, but eventually I've had a surfeit of artificial company and I turn everything off. I fall back onto a chair, dust rag in hand, chin on chest, and blue-jeaned legs outstretched. The music, the voices, leave no echoes. The day steps forward for my attention; I watch water drops worming across the windowpane.

The mist is still floating across the hills; on the fields, snow recedes from islands of tawny grass. The afternoon grows dark around the edges, imperceptibly, as if a lid is being lowered very slowly onto a box. I go to the telephone and call Peter, ask him to come in from the studio, suggest we go for our daily walk. I hang up, wondering what Jake is doing. I think about all the people I love; how they are *somewhere*, at this moment, thinking and breathing; how I could connect myself with them by picking up the phone, and yet, at the same time, how, in the empty house, I feel compelled to listen to the silence—to feel my aloneness, to sense a sorrow that spikes my heart like the spruce trees, cloaked, revealed.

ॐ

MARCH 29, 1995: *I'm waiting for a lot of things. To have the vision to be able to return to my writing. To want to photograph. For my manuscript to be accepted or not accepted. For a peaceful heart, simple happiness. And to give up the need to control. At lunch, today, P and I talked about how we have a new desire: not to care. I think this means not to strive. Not to make things happen, but to let things happen. We talked about this, and about Jake, about his memories of his childhood, about how he perceives us, about what he may do with his life. It seems that this is the central thing that is happening to us: this examination of our lives; our recent past, our present. Our work, suddenly, seems unimportant. And I have such sorrow in my heart. I get used to it, and yet every once in a while I take it out and examine it. It is to do with losing one part of my life—the passage of time within which I'm a mother of a growing child—and the fear that I'm at an ending, with no beginning in sight.*

ॐ

When we go out, the fog is so dense that the barns loom and then vanish as soon as we head out into the fields. We follow a row of red pines. There's no sound but our boots thudding, our jackets swishing. We head up the hill, turning away from the pine trees; soon they, too, vanish, and then I can see nothing: not hills, although I know the ravine-cliff is just over there, not hedgerows or rocks, nothing but a white fog that swallows sound, sight, and space. Peter, five paces ahead, trudges into the gloom as in photographs of climbers on Mount Everest. I call out to him that we could get lost here on our own place. He walks on, totally unconcerned, calling back that we couldn't get lost even if we tried.

Well, yes. I could find the pine trees and follow them home like a line of crumbs. Peter disappears. I hear his footsteps, fading. I'm in a landscape of vapour. I'm afraid, suddenly, of our dependence upon one another; and aware, as if for the first time, of how I need to pay attention to our friendship, treat it tenderly, as I would any living creature.

THE BOWL

Six weeks from the day I sent it out, my manuscript returns.

It's a bleak weekday in early April. I walk to the mailbox. Our mail arrives in a bundle secured with a heavy rubber band, and I always unsnap the band and shuffle through flyers, bills, orders, and manila envelopes, aware of expecting surprises at either end of the emotional spectrum: unimaginable news that will be glorious or devastating. There it is, a bulky mailer with the publisher's name like a flag flying over a country that refuses me entrance. I rip it open, take out a form letter. *This is not the type of material we are looking for at present.*

I drop the mail on the kitchen table. Peter is pouring water into a teapot. He looks up, not at me, but at the mail. Mail, for all our lives here, has been as important as the telephone. Soon it will fade in importance, replaced by computer screens. I grimace, wave the manila envelope. As I go upstairs with it, needing to examine it further, in private, I hear his worried, encouraging voice. "There's more than one fish in the sea . . ."

A form letter.

How can it mean so much? A friend once told me that I would be the same person, to her, whether or not what I wrote was published. I don't try to explain how something inside me is slowly fading. Life falls away behind me, in thousands of tiny losses. Time falls like water, wearing away my life, and I ache for what I can't save. My writing is like a wild bird's egg found in a nest of grasses. I turn from person to person, cupping it in my hands, but they talk to one another, avidly, and no one sees what I'm offering.

❦

Last fall we heard chainsaws. There's a plantation of jack pine up in the hills, so we thought it was being harvested. Peter went up to check and returned white-faced with rage. Two beloved spots on the edge of our farm had been clear-cut: one, the plateau we call The Lookout; and the other, one of our most treasured places, The Bowl.

The Bowl is the first place where spring wildflowers appear. It's a steep-sided valley formed by a tiny rivulet that makes its way beneath maples and birch, tumbling down, at its end, in five or six miniature waterfalls and merging with a larger brook. The ground is soft and rich, a sweet-smelling humus of decayed leaves. Maples cast shadows over fern beds. The hills on either side of the rivulet are carpeted, in early May, with spring-beauty, white flowers with rose-veined petals. Warmth settles into The Bowl. The water makes a cool trickling, blending with the trills of robins and white-throated sparrows. Maples brush the sky with tasselled buds, and the yellow spurs of Dutchman's breeches, like upside-down pantaloons, stir on translucent stems. Beside the brook, fiddleheads arch, fat braids bursting their papery skins. A faint drift of green—trilliums, white violets, the speckled leaves of trout-lily—trembles over the quilt of snow-sodden leaves. We walk in the brook, stepping from stone to stone, so our feet won't crush the flowers.

After Peter brought the news, Jake went up to the woods. He returned with the grim expression of a person contemplating the site of a burned house. "Desecration" was all he would say.

All winter I haven't gone near the clear-cuts. On the day that my manuscript returns, I walk up the ridge trail. Ahead, through the trees, I see emptiness where once there was an etching of branches. The sky is white, bleak. I brace myself and step forward into the place where the path once wound into an open forest of maples, a cathedral-like clearing where I'd always gone to quiet my heart.

I'm in a clear-cut, and now I can see all the way up to the top of a hill I never knew existed. I can see the blueberry barrens. The fold that we called The Bowl is only that—a fold; a gully running down through a desolation. The sides are littered with the tops of trees—like great, flung brooms. Nothing has any relationship to anything else. The land seems to have been stirred, whisked, flayed. Roots gape. Stumps are raw. I stumble forward through the slash, spruce boughs clinging to my jeans, maple branches entangling my feet like mattress springs. *Where is it?* Where's our slender, trodden trail? Our dead birch clad in maze-gill fungi? The patch of turkey-tails? Or the place where the hay-scented ferns caught the red leaves? The squirrel's nest? The hollow where the Indian pipe grew, year after year?

I sit on a stump.

I have to make myself look at this mess. I can't go on pretending it isn't here. The place blurs, the heat of my love for it swims across my vision. The rage is familiar, yet it's futile. Nothing makes me understand that better than sitting in this place whose familiar shape has vanished.

I sit looking out across the wasteland. I can't identify any of our landmarks, the places that taught us how to navigate this land. The road map is gone. I have no choice but to see it exactly as it is.

WILD AS A BLEEDING TWIG

Kevin and Patricia have been making maple syrup. Peter and I walk up the hill road after supper to watch them boil down the last batch of sap.

Snow-melt is coming off the hills; cold mist on the evening air smells earthy. I step over rivulets; there are fissures in the mud, and frost pockets quake like bogs beneath our weight. Along the edge of the road, a fish-grey freshet comes rushing and tumbling down. It's a child's paradise. Halfway up the hill, we leave the road and follow a path through the trees. Children's voices ring through the air, unintelligible and yet familiar. The path emerges in a field that spreads across the steep hillside. Up at the top, in the trees, there's an old wood stove. Smoke rises from its pipe. Wood is stacked under a tarp, and paths trampled into the blue-cold forest snow lead back to the big maples.

Crossing the field, we crunch through archipelagos of thin snow and then stride over brown grass. The woodsmoke belongs to the cold spring air like fiddleheads in a pail.

The four boys come running down to meet us, trying to out-shout each other. The two youngest know they are going to be up past their bedtime, know they'll be outside as the stars come out in the blue-black sky high over their house. We go up to the wood stove where Kevin and Patricia are tipping sap from buckets into a stainless-steel double sink that serves as an evaporator. Steam swirls from the boiling sap. The oldest boy begins sawing a spruce log into pieces. He's absorbed in his important task. Wet sawdust and needles cling to the Swede saw, cover his wool mittens. The door of the wood stove stands open, and Zane squats, poking in a stick.

I squat next to him. Heat parches my cheeks. The young boy takes me into his presence without invitation. He assumes that I, too, will see the fact of this magic and be amazed by the way the stick comes alive, changing from wood to pulsing fire.

In the long spring evenings, light fades from the sky with the same lingering seduction as the calling of the snipes, high over the valley; the sound of running water comes more distinctly, as does the smell of mud and fringed catkins, black and stirring on night breezes. Over us, branches vein the sky, intricate as coral. A few stars glimmer through the budded twigs. They don't pierce the sky like the stars of winter but seem close, as if their silver light reflected the leaping brooks.

Clank of pail handle; a bucket of sap hampers the legs of the seven-year-old, who hauls it two-handedly. Patricia tips it into the evaporator. The front batch of sap is nearly boiled down. The children run down the field like a flock of birds, chasing their wild exhilaration with arms outstretched, as if it were something they might catch. Watching them, I remember spring evenings of my own childhood, running through earthy dusk after a winter of sitting cramp-legged at a desk—no coat, no mittens, cool-edged air on my belly. And in the warm, frog-pulsing night—*light from bedroom window, shadows, lilac bush, bat's flicker*—sensing how the bursting buds and pollen were as reckless as my own exuberant growth.

I sit on a log by the stove, feeling a strange, sweet ache.

We chew on twigs. The air is moist and cool, and the green wood hisses on red coals. We talk about raspberries and Rototillers. We wait for the syrup.

Around us the trees are supple with sap. They're like whales or seabirds. Pods, flocks, forests: they move together, trees in a wind, whales in a pod, compelled at the same instant, responding to the same necessities. A wind comes up the field and the maple branches whish, make a soft sighing, rather than the brittle rattle of winter.

Kevin, freckle-faced, red-haired, wearing a sweater with frayed elbows, slides the ladle into the sap, lifts it carefully, and offers it to me. The steam rising from the pan is sticky, smells of earth and bark. I take the wood handle in my leather mitt. Before I sip, a breeze touches my face with the forest spice of spruce resin, melting snow, and damp earth.

It's the light, the light coming back, that awakened the sap, that melted the snow, that will quicken the frogs.

The syrup tastes of wet bark, of smoke. I close my eyes, take another sip. Essence of spring. Wild as a bleeding twig, clean as wind, the thin syrup holds a promise within it of a deeper sweetness to come.

EARLY APRIL

I'm alone for a week. Jake's away at French camp; Peter is taking work to galleries and visiting his parents. In the big house, I'm neither wife nor mother.

On this spring morning, when I awaken to solitude, the house is warm. I loaded too many logs in the furnace and, at this time of year, the dry wood burns fast and makes a fierce heat. Curled in my bed-nest, I stare at my slippers. They lie just as I left them last night, toes touching. The morning song of birds is remote beyond the storm window. The windows have not been opened since October. No breeze has stirred the parrot feathers on the mantelpiece. Dust gathers on a robin's egg.

The sun shifts endlessly northward; the skylight over the stairs angles a beam directly onto my face. Warm, dust-dancing, the light's wild origins are domesticated by curtains and furniture, and yet, as if the out-of-doors has made its way into my bedroom, sunlight seeps into my brain, alters my patterns.

Outside, in the mud-sweet air, nothing questions or resists the imperative of growth. I listen to the faint sound of the birds, removed from me by insulated walls and two panes of glass. Under my blankets, I'm mired in a season that has passed.

❧

Quiet has many qualities. When there are other people in the house, sunlight holds the texture of their dreams, of their warm and tossed bedclothes; their energy is palpable. This morning, every sound—the rattle of the bathroom doorknob, the dripping shower—is magnified by the fact that no one else hears it. I stand, towel in hand, listening. A fly buzzes, and its body taps against window glass. I notice the drone of the refrigerator. I can imagine what the dog is doing by the clicking of her toenails.

In the kitchen, I plug in the teakettle and stand at the table, cutting a slice of bread from the loaf. On this same table, I have made blueberry pies with my niece, playdough animals with my son. I've leaned on my elbows and looked across its knife-scarred maple into the faces of friends. I've cleared it of beer bottles after parties. I've potted tomatoes on it. I've covered it with packages of seeds, with mittens and ice-crusted mufflers, with piles of dinner plates. I've worked at it for twenty-five years, vigorous in my roles. They are roles that I imagined, and yearned for, as a child. *Someday. Someday I will own a house, run a business, be a mother.* I embraced the future as if life stretched ahead interminably.

&ॐ

APRIL 1, 1995: *Helped Judith in her café last night. Her dishwasher had called in sick. I, Judith, and the two wait-staff were dressed entirely in black, with black aprons. I felt as if we were Italian widows, but with our hair caught back in colourful scarves. Rain-streaked windows, condensation on the inside. Crumpled napkins, loud laughter. A blues band. Sliding through a crowd carrying a tray, I thought how nice it is to feel part of something larger. Helping, adding my skills, quietly.*

Self-worth: the need to get a grade, to make the "A" on the paper, in order to believe in myself. That is outside affirmation. Where is my own yardstick? What is it about myself that I like, that I care about, that I believe is good? What is the basis of self-love from which I can give love? It's time for me to learn that I'm the only one qualified to judge myself.

Alone, for a week. Saw a racoon, waddling in the brook, happily (it seemed) splashing.

&ॐ

After breakfast I get the ladder from the barn and climb onto the porch roof, treading cautiously, since the steel roofing is slippery with birch catkins. I look into my bedroom. From this vantage point of watery wind, it looks static, like a dusty bouquet of dried flowers. I bang loose the storm window's rusty turn-latches with a hammer and ease the cumbersome window down across the sill. Dead flies fall from their winter's tomb and scatter on the breeze.

That night, I put an extra quilt on my bed and shove the window wide open. I drift into sleep listening to the sound of water—the splashing, trickling, and pouring of all the rivulets that vein the bottomlands. Everywhere, the earth is being released. In the ravine, blue-green icicles drip like leaky faucets until the brook overflows its banks, runs over the bridge, carries an entire small spruce tree down from the woods and maroons it in the middle of the pasture.

I awake, on the second morning of my aloneness, to the chirling of swallows, the chinking of blue jays. They are so close, so intimate. They have no idea I am here. Air crosses the sill and sets the paper lampshade swaying. It brings the raw outdoors into my room: dew-spangled crocuses; soil; the manure pile, thawing.

I throw back the covers and swing out of bed all at once, my mind one instant ahead of my body as if my imagination, like the birds, has returned. I go directly downstairs and open the kitchen door. The air is cold, but I want the house to breathe, to come alive. I want the parrot feathers to blow off their shelf.

I stand in the back door under the tattered remnants of spider webs, steam swirling from the hot coffee in my mug, sun on my face. In the clear light of morning I cradle my cup in two hands and recognize a familiar person, wind blowing her hair, wanting to dig in the garden—*me*.

APRIL 2, 1995: *I imagine myself as an old woman, my body's integrity eroding in frightening increments. Living alone—Peter gone, friends dying. As I saw happen to my grandmother, who told me,*

when she was eighty-two, that her days passed ever more slowly while the years flashed by. I feel it beginning, this old person's sense of time. How can it be another season, so soon? Yesterday, when I put my shovel to the soil, I had the strange feeling that I had just recently finished preparing my garden for winter. I said to myself: you can't not make a beginning, just because you can already see the end.

❧

I dig along the permanent pea fences. The fences are heavy page-wire, stapled to stakes. Some of last year's vines wrap around the rusty wire; I can crunch them to powder. Rotting hay, horse manure, eggshells, coffee grounds, cabbage leaves: every year I fold forkfuls of crumbly compost into the reddish dirt and see the soil turn chocolate brown. Today, as I make trips down the garden's centre path pushing a wheelbarrow-load of compost, I'm thinking about how I've been living between two imaginary worlds: the past—people and places stuck in memory like pressed roses—and the future—looming before me like an exam for which I must prepare. But perhaps past and future are like eggshells and seeds. They decay, feed, propel—make the loam of the present.

Everything is active in the starting of the day. I'm surrounded by birds that fly low, trailing bits of dead grass in their beaks; by baby spiders, crawling over the warm hay in the perennial bed; by worms, beetles, maggots. Just across the pasture, schools of trout shimmer in the brook; frog eggs spawn in the pond. I love the morning light: it's shimmery, silver as water; whereas, after lunch, the light gathers density and begins its decline. I poke wrinkled, pale pea seeds into the warm loam. *Must middle life be like the noon of a day? Why should I live braced against the passing of time?* The sun is warm on my shoulders. My mind eases into the rhythm of my task. No one sees me. No one waits for me. The day stretches ahead.

My life is like the soil of this garden—endlessly transforming, in need of a dose of compost every once in a while.

DARK FLOWER

On my last solitary day, I rise before dawn, pull on jacket and wool gloves. Socks cushion my feet inside knee-high rubber boots. I stride up over the fields. Pearls of dew tremble on wild strawberry leaves. There are pink clouds in the east. The unlit trees are motionless.

My path winds through drenched spruce trees. I scramble up a steep slope and come out above the waterfall. Like a foraging woodchuck, I wander along the brook as it chatters through an open wood of maple and beech. Shafts of sunlight quiver; tree trunks hold warmth.

Alone, in spring. I wake alone and speak to no one. I walk in my own rhythm, think my own thoughts. Nothing seems urgent. I step into an empty place inside myself, filled with light.

The spring flowers are so tiny that you could slide down the steep hillsides and destroy hundreds with your boots without knowing it. They're here for only a few weeks. They push up through the brown mat of undisturbed leaf-fall: white violets in a damp pocket beneath a log; yellow trout-lilies, their leaves mottled.

The brook water breaks over rocks, makes pools where submerged leaves exhale silver beads. Its murmur, a thread of morning, weaves with the rush of wind through the red-budded maples, with the fingering light that washes up over stones and shines along the coiled ferns.

There are flowers everywhere I look. Clusters of violets growing in mud. Trillium, their stems piercing the leaf mat. I kneel, put a finger under a blue violet. One tiny flower face, with translucent petals, a tuft of beard, and veins like a lion's whiskers.

Beauty is an ache, a presage. A glimpse, a longing, and a bewildering ecstasy.

꩜

APRIL 3, 1995: *Walked in the woods this morning. All around me the forest was being reborn, life spreading its irrepressible tide over the winter's remnants. Every seed, every root, has its impetus. Spring comes, rampantly. Its purpose is to be. To be is to have purpose. These flowers do not grow to be admired. If I had not come today, no one would have seen them, not even once. No one would love them. No one would mourn their passing. No one would remember them. They stir on the air, as if they're dancing. All I have, all I can ever hold onto, is me, alive, in this moment. Me, growing with the same relentless energy as this spring forest. Me, on this leg of my journey.*

I turn from the brook and start up a steep slope, my leg muscles flexing, my boots digging into the soft soil.

Peter and Jake are returning today. I feel the unfolding of my love for them pushing through the detritus of my crumbling walls like some dark flower.

KILLDEER

By late April the living room is finished. The new floor-to-ceiling shelves are filled with books. The floor is glossy with a fresh coat of urethane. We bought a green leather couch and a chair to match. We had our old couch reupholstered with white canvas. It snugs into the southwest corner of the room, strewn with African mud-print pillows, already flattened by the curve of my spine and the imprint of my head. I've made a nest in the corner of this couch. My wicker knitting basket lives there; it's like a pincushion, both yielding and repellant, spiky double-pointed needles holding a half-finished mitten amid twists of cream-coloured wool. On a pine coffee table is an empty wineglass, a telephone, a book hooked with a pen. At the end of the couch is a small shelf filled with books that have landed there at particular seasons of our lives and never been filed. They're still potent, like books in a store: Nelson Mandela's *Long Walk to Freedom, Three Ways of Asian Wisdom, The Education of Little Tree.*

❧

APRIL 27, 1995: *For the first time in ages I feel the need to write. It's like an ache in my heart. The privacy of writing: I feel as if a wall has crumbled inside me, a wall that closed me off from other people. Hidden behind that wall was the person I wanted to be, my own real self, a self I could show people only with my writing. Now I begin to feel that I can be that person—open, unafraid. Thus the desire to create comes from a new place, for a different reason. Remember, this is who you are—not only a still and listening mother whose job is to tend a child's wounds. Consider your own darkness, your own light.*

Jake is so busy with the school play that we hardly see him. He breezes through the house. It's still his, this house, and yet he seems like a visitor. I think he's beginning to see us, now, almost with surprise, like people he's meeting for the first time.

Temporary lull in the studio. I should go up to my study but am sitting here on the couch, absorbing the fragility of desire and dream, breeders of illusion. Last week I spoke to a man in the aisle of the grocery store. His intelligent eyes looked into mine, and he laughed. He spoke of spring, wondered how his garlic had fared over the winter. Today he is dead—he hanged himself in his barn. Lord! It's been a week of killings and despair. Children have murdered children in a school cafeteria. Species vanish. Families in war zones gather belongings in blankets and flee their homes. At chorus rehearsal a friend said to me, "How could anyone choose to bring a child into this world?" A light seems extinguished, like dawn, whose arrival we've always counted on.

I have sent out my manuscript again.

❧

It's the end of winter, but today it doesn't feel like the beginning of spring. Sitting on the couch, in the living room, I can't hear the wind, although pussy willows bounce insouciantly on yellow-skinned branches just outside the window. I think of the years when Peter and I were young and our future seemed lustrous, unshaped, loose as a glossy pelt. Now the world seems like a once-loved book I have read so often it has lost its allure.

I watch the pussy willows, which must be making swishing sounds, like whips, and feel a twitch of energy. I stand and stretch, call the dog. "Walk?" Immediately she answers me, her toenails making a joyful scrabble as she frolics in place. Together we'll go out to see what is happening in the sweeping air.

I'm surprised, when I step out the back door, to find that the weather has changed. It's no longer bleak—the sky has cleared, and clouds sail up from the southwest, serene and majestic as ships. Their underbellies are grey, but their shifting, piling tops are white, sun-filled. The spruce trees on the northern slopes darken as the clouds move across them and, at the same time, the fields lighten, as if they are illuminated, and I see that beside every blade of bleached grass is a tiny green one.

I walk up over the field and stop at the opening in the hedgerow. The sun is hot on the nape of my neck. The only sound is the chirp of robins; they seem remote, off in their own world in the wispy pasture grass up past the oat field. Their wings glint as they hop from spruce tree to juniper bush. In the field, young timothy and clover make a green mat between the rows of stubbly oat stalks. The sky seems high, higher than a winter sky. It's a sky that feels released, like a vast cloth let loose to billow and dry, held tenuously at the corners. I stop at the dirt lane and look back; over the field, tiny in the watery sky, two white-bellied swallows come sheering over the pines, their wings angled, and they collide in mid-flight, touch, and cut away.

I've decided to go up the Hammond Brook to look for fiddleheads, bursting like violin necks from the black river soil.

By the time I've reached the edge of the woods, I've taken off my jacket and tied the arms around my waist. Long ago, spruce trees sprouted at the edge of a hayfield, and it's warm in the pockets between them. Patches of granular snow, melting, exude wintery air. An orange butterfly darts at me, flutters around my legs, flies off over sprawling blackberry vines. The wind rises like an intaken breath and then sighs; the supple spruce boughs lift and drop, graceful as horses' necks. I branch onto a path that weaves between alders, cuts through a thicket of young fir— rabbit territory—and emerges in hardwoods where sunshine in soft, budded branches, high above, makes me stop and look up. A torn strip of birch bark stirs, glows like a tiger lily. Traversing a bog on a slippery log, I pass the place where I found the marshhawk feathers. I skirt the hollow where jack-in-the-pulpits will appear in June, and I arrive at the river.

The headwaters of this river are somewhere up past our boundary, beyond the blueberry barrens. The river's source is a mystery, but I've seen its ending as it nears the sea, so swollen that it moves almost without seeming to, sliding in black curves through marshlands. Here in our woods the river is still a brook, three big steps to the other side, where a steep hill, covered with birch trees, boulders, and evergreen ferns, blocks the winter sun and keeps the valley cool in summer. The brook tumbles over rocks and sandy shallows, flashing with spring light: hard, sharp, filled with energy.

I'm drawn to its pools. They are formed by windfallen trees that channel the water into small cascades. I stand watching water slide over a submerged log whose polished wood is golden as newly minted pennies. The water shatters, then breaks into green and silver bubbles that spin deep in the pool's heart, before joining the amber stillness.

I'm at a place where a spring freshet comes down from the hills and runs into the bigger brook. It's a rivulet that runs only in winter and spring, and it leaves a mossy stair in summer. I listen. All I can hear is the long rushing of waters, one theme broken by breaks and checks, a sunlit splash here, a rock-thrusty spill there.

The snows of winter are vanishing, rising as mist from shadowed hollows, falling in sudden slides from cliffs. I feel as if the forest is spring cleaning: like horses, belly-up, kicking the clouds to press their withers into the warm soil; men on ladders lifting storm windows from casings, or women washing curtains and spreading sheets on new grass; children, running, wind in the grooves of their spines.

The woods are shedding, emptying themselves of what is over and finished, as if this ending is the true beginning.

I feel something in myself coming loose.

I walk up the path and then squat, lift some decaying leaves, soft as blackstrap; a red root snakes through the black soil. I trace its source to a maple key's bulb, that bisected claw that, as children, we split open and wore on our noses. A brilliant red spider, the size of a pinhead, scuttles over the root. Threading the damp leaves are long purple filaments laddered with embryonic flowers. Everywhere, there are tiny ferns, like sea-horses.

The world's heart is never still.

❧

That night, Peter and I sleep with our window open, blankets piled over duvet, hot-water bottle at our feet. The cold air fingers my face, brings the smell of water as I'm falling asleep.

Later, I'm awakened by the cry of a killdeer. I lie listening, waiting for it to come again. It's the voice of spring, of beginnings. It's mate calling mate, seeking. The cry is urgent, wild, and I imagine speckled eggs in soft grass and drift back to sleep, the night sounds holding me like some great nest.

UNTANGLING BURRS

Today Jake was accepted to art college in Halifax. He's not surprised, and he seems mildly annoyed by how thrilled we are.

"Oh my God, Jake," I say, flipping through the papers. "This is so great."

He sits in the rocking chair by the window, reading *The Fellowship of the Ring.*

"Jake?"

He looks up. Our enthusiasm, I realize, is like intrusive

music. When he was younger he said to us, once, dryly, "I'm not your pet dog."

Peter leans against the edge of the kitchen table, ankles crossed. Sometimes I think we're parodies of our younger selves. We're battered by time but don't realize it. Peter has a few silvery hairs at his temples. He's reading through the bottom of bifocals, although he wears glaze-spattered jeans, running shoes, and a sweatshirt.

"No residence. We'll have to get over right away to look for an apartment."

Jake returns to his book. This is his concern, but his dad is gathering it up eagerly, planning, envisioning. Once, an argument would have brewed. Now I see that Jake is ignoring his father.

"When do you want to go over?" Peter is thumbing through his organizer.

"Jake?" I say.

He looks up.

"Congratulations."

"Thanks, Mum."

Peter looks up. There's a pause, like a sudden turn in a path when our steps falter and we assess what lies ahead.

"Yeah," Peter says, his voice gentling. "Good work, Jake."

By the time I leave for the barn, Jake has put his book down and come to the kitchen table. He and Peter are looking through the materials that arrived in an enormous padded envelope.

I've decided to untangle Minnie's mane. I put her in cross-ties. She stands in the barn facing the open door, manila ropes clipped to each side of her halter. She's black with a white blaze down the middle of her face. Her mane and tail have red tones, as if they've been highlighted with henna. Her eyelids grow heavy with pleasure as I separate the hairs of her mane, tugging at the burrs that she's picked up—or, rather, that have chosen her as their carrier. They've clung for months, persistent as new ideas. They're winter burrs, brown, but their hooks remain strong, barbed at one end. Each one is filled with seeds that will spill whenever they're wrenched loose. Last winter I attempted to comb Minnie's mane and became overwhelmed by the twisted hanks of hair, the rolled knots.

I run my hand down her bony face. "Sorry, Minnie. I should have done this a long time ago."

A few swallows have returned. They swoop through the door without slowing, rotating their streamlined bodies. In the shadows of the eaves their wings flurry, and they drop to their mud-nests. They wriggle their square shoulders, settling. Their long, forked tails scissor shut, and they make a twittering chatter. *Zip-zip-zip kvick-kvick.* In the confines of the barn, their voices cross and spiral, noisy as people at a kitchen party.

I pinch a burr between thumb and finger, then snip the hair surrounding it with the looped handles and beaklike blades of Chinese scissors. The hank of hair is matted and dusty as I tug it apart. It's like a net, criss-crossed. There's no obvious way to disentangle it, so I pull it sideways, diagonally, up and down, small persistent tugs until it separates. I dig the teeth of a comb into the hair and slide it down.

The peepers are chiming, and evening light reddens the raspberry canes. Garlic, planted last fall, rises in neat green rows. Jake comes out the back door, whistling. There's a new spring in his step, his shoulders are easy, straight, and he picks a rock from the driveway and casts it skyward. Minnie pricks her ears. In the stall, the white pony pokes her head over the boards, crunching hay. I press another burr to my collection, the size, now, of a croquet ball. Already, the mane is halfway done—and its loveliness, and Minnie's pleasure, and Jake's happiness make me calm.

Last week our employee, Sue, gave notice. We're still absorbing the implications of this change. She is indispensable. We've often wondered what we would do without her cheerful presence, her competence, her commitment to quality—as strong as our own. Peter seems uncertain, suddenly, set adrift, as we realize that the pottery business is unravelling, one thread at a time. I see him come out the door after Jake. They compete, for a while, their bodies bent, arms back, flinging rocks.

I draw the comb through Minnie's mane. Already, it's late spring, and the days are lengthening. At 8:30 it will still be vaguely light. Peter goes into the garage. I hear metallic bangings as he works on the tractor.

After I've groomed both horse and pony, I turn them out into the pasture. Minnie flicks her tail as if enjoying its glossy swish, and its red tints gleam, sleek as the raspberry canes. When I go into the kitchen, the air has the faintest earthy scent, like wild violets. Peter and Jake took down the storm doors last Saturday, and now wind sweeps through the house. I go into the dining room, whose north door stands open onto the screened-in porch. One step and I'm standing on its green-painted floorboards, seeing, through the screens, daffodils and the glint of river in the pasture.

I go back through the house. In the blue living room my knitting basket, like the skis hanging in the front hall, belongs to winter. I'll be tucking it behind the couch for the summer. I go upstairs and pass through the door that opens onto my study.

Beneath a skylight are wide shelves holding books, camera equipment, and mat board. In the north wall, another small door leads to the attic and the back stairs. Next to my light table is a tall, closed cupboard filled with slides, filed by year and subject matter. Snug in the southeast corner, next to a narrow window, is my desk.

〜

MAY 1, 1995: *It's not so much that I want to think, or read, or learn, or study as that I want to visit the darkness inside me where something is germinating. All winter I've been sensing this place. It occurs to me that it is not the words I might write that make me who I am. It is the time spent in that fecund darkness.*

When I bend over my light table, squinting through my loupe at a slide and seeing the red sweeping lines of an amaryllis petal, I feel the same awe that I felt looking through the lens of my camera. It's a stirring within a stillness. It's a feeling that I long to save. It abides in the minute space that hovers between pen and paper, finger and shutter.

〜

Isn't this enough? I look around my room. There's the pile of drafts of the manuscript I've just mailed out. There are five fat notebooks filled with slides for gardening books. There are small, brown, spiral-bound notebooks, bent by their journeys in the pockets of my jean jacket, their pages covered with pencilled descriptions of nests, ferns, wildflowers. Gradually, my projects have taken over and now fill an entire room of the house, when once I had only a desk in the corner of the living room.

I sit at my desk, remembering how Peter and I dreamed of a pottery studio and were moved by images of sun-warmed raspberries in stoneware bowls, tea poured from a handmade pot into salt-glazed mugs. Now the pottery business has become like the cow stanchion I once, in a dream, carried on my shoulders. Heavy, hinged, it dragged behind me, tripped me. I threw it in a ditch and began to run. My feet lifted from the ground.

&

A few days later, Peter and I are up at the sauna bath. We've had two more work bees with Kevin, Patricia, and the boys, and the renovation is almost complete. Peter is building the stairs to the second storey, and I'm stripping bark from a tamarack log that lies on the ground. With the point of a knife I pry at the bark, loosen it from its grip on the wood beneath. It's like pulling the tab of a box of laundry soap. Suddenly it releases and begins to strip back. My gloves are sticky with resin. I stand with the end of the bark in my hands and walk backwards, tugging. Beside me on the ground is a pile of bark strips, tangled as old leather reins.

It's May 7th, a Saturday morning. The brook braids through the greening pasture. A cow is in heat and makes a primal, monotonous mooing, the sound blending with the chirp of robins, the splash of water, and the ringing of Peter's hammer.

I love the fact that he's taken time away from the studio and we're working together, outside, as we did when we first came here. And I love the stairs he's building. Its steps are wide, two inches thick, made of freshly milled wood. Unlike the notched log of our original sauna bath, with its rope railing, these stairs will make it easy to trot up to the sauna's changing room, carrying bathrobe, Thermos of tea, change of clothes. Lately, as we try to decide what we're going to do about the business once Sue leaves, we've been looking back on our young selves, bemused. I dig the point of my knife into the bark, pull up another long strip. The exposed wood glistens, smooth and beaded with moisture, like the butter I made when we had a Jersey cow. I made butter, cheese, applesauce, dozens of frozen pies, blueberry preserves, a winter's worth of jam. Every week I made six loaves of bread, baked in a stove whose temperature wouldn't rise because of imperfectly dried wood. We washed our clothes in a wringer washer, mowed our lawn with a cast-iron push mower, and planted enough potatoes to feed four families. There was not a single soft chair in the house; we used upturned logs for dining-room chairs, causing complaints from the older men in the family. We rose at five and went to bed at midnight, never sitting down except to eat. So many things we did either disproportionately or with an enthusiastic embrace of discomfort. Now we're shedding old ways of doing things.

There's nothing wrong with making steps that are wide and strong. There's no reason why I shouldn't have a writing cabin. Still a small voice inside me asks whether I really deserve a place of my own. I feel like someone who's stepped forward from the chorus and offered to sing a solo. Is my voice strong enough? Yet

I want to hear it—a singular voice, my own, not meshed within the pottery production, not merged in family. *Family.* It, too, changes. My mind, like a compass needle, quivers, sensing an attraction. I wonder whether we'll have a *quiet* house, rather than the empty house I've been dreading. Jake knows it's time to leave, yet his childhood seeps from him, makes him restless, brooding. He writes poems, so beautiful that I cry when he reads them to me. I imagine the day we return from leaving him in Halifax. I'll go to my desk and write in my journal. *Took J to Halifax, yellow leaves on the city trees, smell of sea air.*

Peter is almost finished. The building is the same shape it always was: a little blockhouse, the top level overhanging the lower. It's like a filthy person emerged from a hot shower— innocent, scoured, renewed. The new timbers gleam: there's a door handle made of a birch branch, and square-sided timbers support an upper-storey porch. The window glass glints.

I've put an ad in the paper. *Wanted: extremely small wood stove.* I found an old table covered with peeling paint. It's in the wood-shop, where I'm sanding it. I'm painting a rocking chair fire-engine red. I bought a red enamelware teapot and two mugs, to match.

The last strip of bark lies on the moss. The stair railing is sticky, sleek, golden, like a newly born creature.

Peter drops his hammer into the ring on his holster. Girls still stare at him and giggle behind their hands, thinking he looks like Mick Jagger, with his wide mouth, the monkey-lines that etch his cheeks. He's lean, restless. I wonder when he'll give up sprinting between studio and house. He opens a hand towards the stairs, gesturing, and I walk up. The steps are just right—the risers not too high, the treads wide enough for security. The stairs neither shake nor creak. They are inviting, and I imagine the moment when I carry up an armload of books, paper, pencils. Peter follows, and we sit cross-legged on the porch, leaning against the sun-warmed siding. We watch the brook. It slides through the grass like an otter, black, quivering with light. It makes low chuckings, trills, slaps. Soon this meadow will fill with blue-flag iris, then with ferns and buttercups.

In this building I'll take sauna baths, and I'll write. The resin-scented wood will hold me as I listen to river-song and wind-mutter—waiting, for sweat, for words.

The people who lived here before us saw, on the north side of the house, a barnyard from which cows, on summer evenings, shambled up a lane. On the hillsides, children carried baskets of wild strawberries, men stooked buckwheat, black Percherons stood patiently before heaped hay wagons. Our minds, however, held no such images. We saw only wind-stirred grass. One day, when Jake was a little boy, Peter and I sat leaning against the side of the house looking up across the fields to the ravine, a rocky headwall rising at the end of a narrow valley. My brother had just phoned to say that he and his wife and two children had to cancel their long-planned summer visit. Their beds had been made, the freezer stocked with casseroles. I'd filled a tin with oatmeal cookies. Desolate, we watched the grass rippling across the hills. The wind was cold, although it was June. At that moment I decided that the field must become a backyard, bound by perennial gardens. Peter envisioned the porch. Our loneliness evaporated, and we turned our minds to creation.

Now, fourteen years later, it's a warm day in May, and I'm on the familiar porch, sitting on a couch hung from the ceiling by chains. My journal is open in my lap. This morning I awoke feeling perfectly balanced and calm. I've seen Jake off on the bus. Peter kissed me, as always, before crossing the yard to the studio, even though I might see him again in a few minutes. And I'm on the porch, with a pen in my hand.

My grandmother is somewhere high in a corner of my mind, like a kite. I tug the string. There's a clear sky, a sustaining wind. Down she comes, smiling. There's a honey jar shaped like an old-fashioned beehive; stairs so steep I have to go up them on hands and knees; the clink of a silver lid; piano, out-of-tune. She lands, like Mary Poppins, and steps forward, into my present, with her arms spread wide.

I lean to my journal and begin to write.

SUMMER

SNIPES, WOODCOCKS, AND PEEPERS

Supper's over, the dishes are in the drainer. Peter and Jake have just rattled past the open window on their mountain bikes. We ate early so they could ride to the Londonderry church and be back before dark. They'll head up the same road we skied last winter, grinding past the blueberry barrens that are quilted, now, with red-leaved bushes bearing white and pink blossoms. They pass beneath the maple trees. I can hear their voices, calling back and forth over the scritching rubble of their tires. I'm happy that they're having some good father–son times.

The phone rings and I pick up the receiver, expecting a call from my mother. But it's not her. It's a young woman with a warm, vibrant voice. She sounds thrilled when I say, cautiously, that yes, this is Beth. She tells me her name. She's an editor at the publishing company where I sent my manuscript. She loves my book.

I tuck the phone between shoulder and chin, find a pencil and a slip of Canadian Tire money on the kitchen table where I scribble her name and phone number. I hang up the phone and stand in the doorway to the sunroom. Then I slide down to the floor, my sneakered feet propped against the frame. I want to feel wedged, held by something strong. My heart is hammering. *Someone has heard me.*

Max, our only cat now, pads into the kitchen. He has a pure

white belly and four white paws. He's so relaxed he seems boneless, and he climbs into my jackknifed lap, circling until I, too, relax and sit cross-legged. He purrs, kneads my jeans.

I think about my writing life, how it began as soon as I learned to read and realized I could continue the story even after I put the book down. Mine was a country childhood, with no neighbourhood of kids, so I talked to myself softly, out loud, continually, until it became a mental pattern. *She went up to the woods. Now it was getting late, so she started home. She put her hand underneath the broody hen, hoping she would not get pecked.* As I whispered my life to myself, I put it in a safe place. Everything was as it was in the real world; there were cows, pillows, willow trees, stars, safety pins, parents. But in my mind they were sharper, brighter, richer. Like the universe, my imaginary world bent round and held itself.

The peepers start up, out by the pond and in the marshes. They begin as soon as the cool of the evening yields dampness. A few tentative cries probe the night, and then, like a band of miniature, mad bell-ringers, shrill cries come teeming as the tree frogs make their mating call, luring females, trying to out-shout one another.

At the same time, I hear another presage to darkness, as the snipes and woodcocks begin their courtships. Both are reclusive, long-billed birds whose cries and daring aerial displays criss-cross the spring evenings. Both make plangent calls, more buzz than song. Their cries are the earliest signs of spring, coming when the fields are brown and soggy, always startling us. They have an eerie familiarity, like a recurrent dream. *Scaip. Scaip.* The snipe makes a nasal buzz. It flies so high it can't be seen, but we hear the hollow, winnowing *woo woo woo* as it dives straight towards the ground, vibrating its outer tail feathers. The woodcocks make a small dark *peent*. Only once, in all these years, have we witnessed the woodcock's wild display, although we often flush the ungainly little birds from reeds. In an abandoned clearing where blackberries sprawl in August, we saw the woodcock come swooping towards the brown grass. Wings partly folded, it rose and fell, every plummet converted to a soar.

Their urgent secrecy is like my writing life. In the obscurity of dusk, when trees, bushes, rivers become less solitary, half-gathered into darkness, the birds and peepers pursue their creative instincts. I, too, have been secretive. No one but I needed to share the stories I scrawled, when I was eight, on blue-lined paper. *Ponies, rocks, and heather. The sea. A stone croft.* I wove fibres of isolation, weather, and self-reliance. Later, when I began to outgrow my childhood, I tried to make its shape: *lilacs, wasps, pear trees, pond hockey, barn fires.* The world, as I saved it, wasn't quite the same, but became more real, like the whispered words. *Hoping she would not get pecked.* Words folded into mystery, like the trees of dusk. And there, in creative dusk, you can hide.

My hand slides over the cat's fur. *I love this book,* the editor said.

That place where you hide can become someone else's, although that was not my motivation when I wrote in my notebook after coming home from school. *How was your day? Oh, fine.* I rested my feet on the rungs of my desk, and for punishment the teacher made me take off my Hush Puppies and tie them around my neck. I went in sock feet all day, wearing the shoes. They bumped my chest and swung into my face in the cafeteria as I carried my lunch tray with its plate of Sloppy Joe. That same teacher struck my friend's knuckles with the edge of a ruler. He made a big farm boy kneel on beans. He made fun of the Finnish boy whose hands were backwards and whose elbows wouldn't bend. My friend Cathy's mother had a black eye. Cathy told me she wished she had a shotgun so she could kill two people: our teacher and her father. *How's school? Fine.* Then I would take my notebook to the boulder, where on the north side the ground was cold and violets grew. *"The ponies galloped on the hard sand. She stood in the water and watched the sun shining in their blowing manes."* No tears fell for the day just past because I was somewhere else, and it was more present to me, with its crying seabirds and thundering hooves, with its Welsh clouds and green sheep-cropped grass, than the cafeteria and my dusty Hush Puppies.

The glass doors of the sunroom are pushed wide open. There, just close. *Peent. Peent.* The woodcock must be in the meadow. The buzzy call is like a raindrop creasing a puddle. The sound slides into dusk, and I know the coming darkness will be alive with soft stirrings, twitchings, unfoldings.

I sit in the doorway, patting the cat, sensing how wind blows through me like the spring breezes that freshened our house. I feel the energy of my own sources.

I want to make sweeping gestures, dance my excitement. I push myself to my feet, shedding the cat, who stalks away with a straight tail.

DOE AND FAWN

At the end of May the wild fruit trees come into flower just when the poplars unfold their gold-green leaves. Cherry, apple, and serviceberry trees appear in hedgerows and hillsides like ballerinas on point, pink skirts wind-stirred. They float, here and there, softening the spruce-clad hills. Light glistens in their petals; wind steals their fragrance.

One morning I go out with my camera before Jake and Peter are awake. As I walk past the cluster of buildings—barns, studio, woodshop—I can smell their damp cedar shingles. The sun rises over the hills; its rays splinter through the spruce trees and splay over the fields, lighting strands of spider silk whose long threads stretch from grass to grass like pieces of fishing line, cast randomly. A breeze rises with the sun, and strawberry blossoms bounce.

I walk up along the farm lane, heading towards the sauna bath. There are only the faintest cart tracks left, sunken beneath sod. Chokecherry bushes crowd the lane's verge, and serviceberry trees, with their slim white blossoms, arch overhead.

I'm walking slowly, feeling peaceful, sun on my right cheek, when I'm startled by a loud, peculiar sound, like a hollow clap. It's a warning, in any language, and I stop.

There, beneath a serviceberry tree, is a doe and her fawn. They're pressed so close together that, seeing them against the light, I'm not sure, at first, whether I'm seeing one creature or two. Then the fawn separates from his mother. He steps towards me as if curious, gazing wide-eyed with black nostrils quivering. The doe makes her clapping snort, stamps her front leg. She takes one taut, threatening step towards me. Then she and the fawn stand perfectly motionless, heads thrown back. Their ears, backlit, are like black wings.

I'm blundering into their morning like an oar cutting water. I'm intimidated but not frightened. I feel an intruder and try to stand as motionless as they do. The doe turns and, in one sleek bound, she's away up the hill, her white tail rising and falling. The fawn bounces after her, but then he breaks away. He seems, like any child, torn between natural impulse and obedience, and he prances down the steepest part of the hill, where we toboggan in winter. I think he's drawn back towards me, aware of my fascination. The doe stands on the brow of the hill, silhouetted against the pearly clouds, and the fawn vanishes into the woods. The doe breaks her rigid stance. She makes a lunging rear, throws up her long front legs, and, in three or four massive leaps, reaches the bottom of the hill. I imagine her circling round, looping, like a spider's lines, to snare her wayward fawn.

Peter and I spend a Saturday at the junior high school. We're helping with a project to raise money for education in a developing country. The kids are fasting for two days. They spent last night in the gym, sleeping on pads. Today they're making kites. Peter, a few other fathers, and the shop teacher have set up tables in the gym with various workstations: precut balsa wood, rolls of Tyvex building paper, glue, staples. I'm helping the students write little stories; we imagine ourselves to be children in a developing country who have no school. They're serious, both boys and girls, when we talk about hungry children. We work in a sheltered courtyard, sitting cross-legged on the ground, and they crouch over their notebooks, plucking the grass at their feet, chewing pencils, suddenly scribbling. The girls have bright yellow noses from sniffing dandelions. I show them how to make dandelion chains. Some of them already know how, some have forgotten. They crawl, avidly gathering flowers. A few of the boys make them too. Strung around the boys' necks, they are soon limp or begin to separate, their stems curling. The girls, however, make chains long enough to wrap around their wrists several times. They put one hand on hip, offer the other cuffed with thick, fuzzy dandelions. They wear pink T-shirts, skin-tight jeans with patches, plastic hairclips in fluorescent colours, chipped nail polish.

By three in the afternoon the stories are written and push-pinned to a bulletin board. The kites are made, and we go out to the soccer field.

The junior high is on a plateau, next to the hospital. The distant hills are hazy. One of the kites rises immediately. Everyone claps; inspired, the kids begin to run, their fragile kites like puppies on leashes, bouncing behind them end over tail, rustling.

I'm watching a young mother. She has two children: a baby sleeping in a stroller and a two-year-old. She has long black hair caught back in a ponytail, and she wears sunglasses. She's slim, strong. She kneels next to the stroller, one hand on its side, jiggling it gently. Her little boy trundles up to her. *Piggyback!* She crouches. He locks his arms around her neck and she reaches back, arms behind her waist. He clings to her, legs clutching, arms tight, and she rocks forward and back, smiling.

I'm drenched in the sensation of young motherhood, when a child's soft, sturdy body is familiar as blood-knowledge, something you've always known, even anticipated, like a part of yourself you'd been missing. In hands, eyes, voice, the grave and tender gestures of motherhood spring to life, and you remember your own mother. *Mother.* How strange, and how thrilling, to realize that you've become one yourself.

I watch the young woman. She is more glamorous than any celebrity, this lovely mother kneeling on the soccer field, sunglasses slipping down her nose and ponytail tugged by her son's fat hand. She and her children might be any nationality, in any circumstance: selling fruit in a dusty Mexican plaza, stranded on a roadside in Afghanistan. Still they would be as they appear to me now, at this moment, under the clear Canadian sky: held within the invisible web of their mutual need and love.

She waves at her husband who arrives with a five-year-old on his shoulders. They're joined by another couple. I glance at these young families, thinking that they are just beginning their journey. I know, as they do not, what it will feel like when they see their child on stage for the first time; when they chaperone a dance, or bake cookies for a sale, or sew costumes, or study a report card, or wait at the closed door of a classroom for a parent-teacher interview. I see their pride, their anxiety, their stern hope, the fragility of their faith in their children's perfectibility.

❦

MAY 28, 1995: *The blessing of a full heart: sitting on the back step last night, J's arm over my shoulder, I wiped away tears as he read another poem he'd written about leaving home. So often, this year, I've felt a space at my side. Years ago, when I was dreaming of being pregnant, I walked down through the field with my hand out beside me, holding the hand of an imaginary child. How can I have had a baby, watched it grow into a little boy, and be, now, sending him away? Long talk, this morning at breakfast, with Peter and Jake—about dreams, art, nature. Seventeen is such a touching age—J is both amazingly mature and amazingly childish. All day I kept pulling myself up short, saying to myself: Why worry? Why be anxious? Enjoy this day. Enjoy everything—lightning, rain, thunder, and peepers.*

As I watch the young mother, I'm remembering hair and fingers, knee-joints and heels; zippers, frozen boot laces, mittens; shivering body wrapped in a beach towel; hands on shoulderblades, the long-roped swing in the barn; dreams, songs, fights, locked doors; challenges coming one after the other, like labour pains, with barely time to breathe in between. The schooling my child has given me, as I learned dexterity: when to yield, when to resist. And now I'm by myself on a soccer field, and Jake's a young man, off with his friends. They're riding their mountain bikes in some dangerous place that I'd be better off not imagining. A new challenge faces me, and I recognize a familiar sensation. My first impulse is overridden by a deeper instinct: *Say nothing; hold back.* Now it tells me: *Let him go.*

My aloneness in this place of families swirls around me like a long, soft coat that makes me feel like a different person. I wonder how many new feelings I'll encounter as I grow older.

No one pays much attention to me. I could leave, and no one would notice. No child would look for me; I have nothing of anyone else's I'm taking care of: no friend's baby's teething ring, no one's jacket or wet shoes. It's just me, here.

And Peter, out there, like a kindly uncle, throwing a kite into the air encouragingly.

We could go now, both of us. No one would mind. I walk towards him.

"Peter! Peter!"

He's all by himself under the sky, watching a boy running down the field with a kite. Then he turns towards me. I have nothing else on my mind but my desire to slide my hand into his, urge him to leave.

HORNET'S NEST

In early June I'm cleaning out the box room, a shed off the main studio. Here we keep all our packing materials: used boxes that might come in handy, unassembled cartons, rolls of bubble wrap, and garbage bags of dunnage—shredded paper, Styrofoam beads.

Outside the window, up in the corner, there's a movement. A hornet is building a nest. Her head rises and falls as she kneads the window with her forelegs, impervious to my watching.

Dozens of cells, like a honeycomb, cling to the glass. Already the nest is the size of a dessert plate, growing in concentric spirals.

It's the work of a single queen. Fertile, she over-wintered, crouched beneath leaf-litter. Now, all alone, she's building this nest. Right now, she's making a dormitory for her workforce, building only enough cells to contain eggs that, in two weeks, will hatch into larvae. She'll feed the larvae for another two weeks, when they'll begin to pupate, evolving into sterile females. When they hatch, the queen will continue laying eggs, but now the females will take over her jobs: food gathering, nest building, and brood tending. In late summer the queen will finally produce eggs that hatch into fertile males and females, who will mate for the sole purpose of producing fertile females. Only these females, or queens, will over-winter. They'll crawl into rock crevices or beneath fallen logs. And so the cycle will begin again. This nest will be blown into tatters.

Last fall I found a hornet's nest in one of the back fields. It looked like an enormous grey balloon, perched in a patch of gone-to-seed goldenrod. In fact, it was firmly spun around three dead raspberry canes Its entrance, the size of a quarter, had a peaked bulge beneath it, like a chin. I broke the canes and lifted the nest in two hands. It weighed almost nothing. Carrying it home, I marvelled at its texture—curving, quilted layers, striped with the subtle hues of all the papery things the hornets had torn into strips, chewed, and regurgitated: grey maple bark, a creamy bit of sodden envelope, golden cedar, rain-blackened cardboard. The layers curved away from the hive, making the nest puffed and dense, layer upon layer insulating the inner cells from the cold. I held it against my chest, cradled in my arms. It rustled as I walked. I added it to my collection of abandoned things: shells, seed pods, quills, snakeskins.

I'm thinking of how many useless things we keep—like these boxes. One day we realize that even though they're still here, we've really abandoned them.

❧

JUNE 6, 1995: *A busy day in the studio. Sue here—she has only one more week, so was trying to do ten times as much as she usually does. I think she's terribly torn—wants to move on in her life, yet regrets leaving this job. Patricia's oldest boy came down with a school project, a table he made in shop. P made a clay banana for him—glazed and fired—which they attached as a drawer handle. Unexpected customers: I took them up to the gallery, a young couple from Winnipeg on honeymoon. Patricia has started to do our books, and she was installing a computer program in the office. Yet, once Sue leaves, and if I withdraw, what will become of this busy, people-filled place?*

I'm reading Hero with a Thousand Faces *by Joseph Campbell. I transcribed a sentence from the book into my journal: "Tragedy is the shattering of the forms and of our attachment to the forms; comedy, the wild and careless, inexhaustible joy of life invincible."*

❧

I go to town to visit a friend in the health centre. He's in a two-person room and has the window bed. The window overlooks the same blue hills I saw last weekend from the soccer field. A curtain separates us from the room's other occupant, but a small girl escapes her parents' notice and comes tiptoeing to the foot of the bed.

"What's wrong with him?" she asks.

Her question startles me. It's so simple, asked with plain curiosity, but I don't know where to start, how much to explain. I'm not sure myself. Recently divorced, his ill-health seems as much a function of unhappiness as of anything physical. Her eyes devour the tubular steel bed, the IV stand, the man who lies motionless beneath the blue blanket, mouth slack, tongue coated with yellow scum. His hands are palm-down on his chest, fingertips not quite touching. An ID bracelet circles one wrist, a needle is taped to the other. It occurs to me that the girl must think he's an old man, with his bloated cheeks, the network of veins on his nose, his thinning hair.

"He needs to sleep," I say.

"But what's wrong with him?"

A parent peers around the curtain, apologizes. The girl ducks beneath the outstretched arm. I wonder if the child can sense the heartache in this room, if it's what attracts her.

My friend makes an abrupt barking sound. His eyes open, but he doesn't recognize me. He rambles, incoherent, and I pick at the words, like unravelling a tangle of yarn, but his eyes close and his mouth falls slack.

Sitting at his side, I'm obeying an ancient impulse. If he wakes, he won't be aware of me. He won't remember my visit. It makes no sense, when I think about it. *He'll never know.* But my heart tells me otherwise.

This is my old friend, who once stooped and helped his own little girl into a car. She reached up with both hands to pat his face. They went to the woods and gathered wild ferns, bloodroot, and trillium for their garden. He and his wife gave parties, and we danced in their living room, drinking beer, while our children played hide-and-seek in the twilight.

Now he lives alone, with furniture whose shabbiness is revealed in its new location.

What's wrong with him? He's shattered, I could have told her. His nest has been torn apart. He has to make a new one. He thinks he doesn't know how. It's why I'm here at his side. There have been faults, cruelties, betrayals, but no one condemns either partner in this broken marriage. Friends marshal: some go to him; others to her. We'll tell them they're loved, keep them alive.

At five o'clock someone else comes to sit with him. I go outside, breathe the fresh air with relief. I stop at a farm stand to buy more annuals for my garden. Its steps are covered with geraniums—red, salmon pink, white. There's a bulletin board with announcements of strawberry suppers, fiddling contests, fresh asparagus. I fill the back of the car with cardboard flats of impatiens and lobelia. I can't wait to get back to my garden. I'm infected with the compulsion to plant.

It's a twenty-minute drive home and I go slowly, enjoying seeing how people have been making their places ready for the brief, blessed summer. Backyard vegetable gardens are coming up in rows: radishes, lettuce, onions. Sunlight glows in the ribs of rhubarb leaves. Lilacs, dark purple nuggets, are about to open.

I drive past a house with a newly painted green porch. A woman stands on a stepladder tucking petunias into a window box. Bleeding heart grows in the shade beneath her lilacs. Beyond, between her house and the next one, fields spread up towards the forested hills, their soil a corduroy of green seedlings. The air smells of cow manure and freshly cut grass.

I leave town and turn onto the road that winds along a broad valley. Five such valleys spiral up from the town; stretches of forest open, surprisingly, onto sunlit fields. I pass pastures where knobby-kneed Belgian foals flail their dust-mop tails as they follow the broad rumps of their dams. Farmhouses are anchored by lines of laundry, and there's a field of dandelions—thousands of yellow pillows, a swell of light.

I turn left onto the dirt road that goes straight uphill, as if into wilderness, but then turns at the crest and plunges back down into our hidden valley.

I put my hand on my chest. *Funny, how feelings lodge in the chest.* Anxiety is hard, heavy, feels inanimate as stone, and takes up so much room that it crowds the lungs. I remember how, last winter, I went to the back door and stood in the freezing air trying to get enough breath. Now my heart feels like soil swollen by warm rain. Each grain expands, pushes away the one next to it. Space grows and, within it, everything loses shape, floats.

Nothing, at this instant, repeats itself, but stays exactly as it is: dust, billowing up from my tires; the steering wheel, juddering under my hands.

Life invincible.

FLEDGLINGS

We forgot to keep the back door shut, and the swallows built a nest in the woodshed. They snugged it close to the ceiling. Peter went to the attic and drilled a small hole so we could lie on the dusty floor, eye pressed to the opening, and be inches away from five nickel-sized heads. We watched the parent swallows stuffing insects into their babies' clamorous mouths. By the end of July the baby birds were barely contained in the dried-mud nest. They squeezed against one another, bulged against the nest's edge like breasts in a tight bodice. They watched us with their shiny eyes as we passed in and out of the house, directly below. Their wide beaks stretched in perpetual smiles. They became our house gods, their loud chittering as much a part of the back entry hall as the smell of firewood, stacked ceiling-high, or the sight of our cross-country skis, parked for the summer.

One day, in late July, the parent birds swooped in and out through the door, perched agitatedly on the top of the wood pile, and flew back outside, chattering. A baby swallow balanced on the edge of the nest like a child nerving itself on a diving board. It did not fly, but dropped. Its wings made short flutterings, then shocked against the air and held, sending the little body upwards through the open door towards the immense light. The four remaining babies shrugged, settling themselves in the unaccustomed space. Urged on by the parents, they teetered, one by one, on the nest's edge. Their first flight was short. Out the door they flew, and over the driveway, and then a short jag up to the telephone wire. Side by side, the little birds sat on the wire. They tipped, caught themselves, hunched their shoulders. The parent swallows raced away, no longer chattering, but intent on their hunting. Perched on the phone lines, the babies ate their first outdoor meal. By late afternoon they were back in their nest.

Day by day their flights lengthened. The energy of hunger was displaced by another imperative. There was no longer a raucous clamour in the woodshed but urgent wing beats, minutely exclamatory. And then they were gone. I walked down the boot hall, pushed open the screen door to the woodshed, and sensed absence. There were the spiderwebs in the door frame. Sunshine lay in slanting parallels, glistened in the delphiniums. The hall was silent, its air motionless. I stood in the back door. Which ones were they? Everywhere, swallows swooped and glided in the morning sky, so easily you would never guess they had just learned to fly.

Sue works her last day. At four o'clock her car rattles away down the sun-baked driveway, as it has for ten years. Dust hangs in the air, settles on the goldenrod. Her tires make a rumble on the loose boards of the bridge. The car slows at the mailbox. It stops for longer than would seem necessary for her to look right, up the hill, or left, down the valley. I wonder if she's second-guessing her decision to leave. Or perhaps she is absorbing the first moments of falling out of a habit.

After supper, Peter and I decide to go for our evening walk and find ourselves wandering towards the studio, where Jake has set up his easel on the deck. He's tipped it so the blood-tinged light slanting over the western hills infuses his canvas. He's painting an enormous man's face. I stand behind, watching. The sure strokes he takes with his paintbrush make no sense to me. I would never think to paint those short dabs of dark green.

Now he's putting black over the green. Eyes reveal themselves, haggard, in the space he hasn't yet touched.

"Hi, guys." He's calm when working. We're part of his balanced present, the place where he's whole. I sense how we fit now. We're a piece of what surrounds him: the clouds, faint ribbings edged with gold; the fields that hold the day's heat; air breathing from the forests. High school folds behind him. He can imagine the room he'll be living in next year. The face he paints is at the centre.

We go into the studio. Sue has left everything as she always does; brushes rinsed, table sponged, sink tidy. She's finished every single pot. They're on ware boards, on a rolling rack. The unfired underglaze colours are bright—brick red, teal blue— the glaze is a pale chalky green. Peter's wheel area, too, is tidy. The wheel head is mopped; sponges, rubber ribs, wooden scribes, calipers, lifters are laid ready to hand, like dentist's tools. In the packing room the clipboard holds two final orders.

Peter sits on a low chair that's lost its back and become a stool. I walk to the north window. In the evening light the rock face at the end of the narrow valley has no features. It's a black slash behind the light-touched trees.

Everything we've done in the last year has pointed us towards this moment. We've been like people on the last leg of a journey: fatigued, uninterested, needing to stop. Needing to go home.

I walk around the room, picking things up, putting them down. Peter stretches with his hands behind his head. He's watching Jake through the window. I follow his eyes. Jake hunches forward, staring intently at his painting, brush suspended. His concentration is like sleep, or hunger, or pain. Peter and I don't look at each other. I wonder if he feels, as I do, a new sense about himself, as if he's looked in the mirror and found that he's changed. Jake teaches us, unwittingly. He makes us see that, at every moment, we are as new as he is. We, too, are growing. We, too, are leaving something behind.

Peter made stools from old iron tractor seats. They were among the peculiar assortment of things we hurled out the door when our first studio burned to the ground. Finally, I stop my distracted pacing and sit on one of these stools. We don't want to admit to each other that we need to be here in the studio on this day of Sue's departure, but we do. We need to slide our minds over its dusty quiet, like stroking a dying cat. We need to be still, just for a while.

Twenty years ago we bought two old leather suitcases, lined them with foam rubber, and covered the rubber with brown corduroy. We wrapped one sample of each of Peter's pots, with a sample of each glaze, in red flannel. The blue glaze was speckled, slightly stippled. There was an oatmeal-brown glaze and an opalescent green. We packed bowls, mugs, vases, and drove to Montreal in winter. Peter had a moustache and a Ho Chi Minh beard. I wore my hair caught at the neck in a plastic tortoiseshell barrette. We wore bell-bottom jeans and hiking boots, and we carried our suitcases down into the dazzling new underground shopping centres. Our catalogue was handprinted on green construction paper, with orange covers. We returned with three orders and totted them up on an adding machine that had square plastic buttons, pleasing to my fingers, and a hand crank that rolled the paper forward. I entered those first orders in blue order books, using round, careful printing. Our first firings were fraught with anxiety and anticipation. I ran from house to studio, carrying Thermoses of tea and homemade cookies to Peter, who balanced on a chair peering into the kiln's molten interior. Cheeks tight with heat, I took a turn squinting through a pane of dark glass, discerning the lip of a mug, a bowl's swell. After the roaring burners had been silenced, we lifted crumbly firebricks so hot that our fingers were burned through leather gloves. Unbricking a layer or two, we skipped a flashlight's beam into the pulsing darkness, seeing, instead of pots covered with pink or white glazes, a flash of blue; red, like a cardinal's feather; egg-brown, with speckles; the gleam of pooled green. There, waiting, lay an entire kiln-load of treasure.

"The old catenary arch kiln," Peter says, as if he's seeing the same progression of images. "The Fundy Park Craft Festival. The store . . ."

It had been a barbershop. Its door was glass with bevelled facets, and there were squares of stained glass over the display window. The rent was eighty dollars a month. We had an unlimited supply of cardboard boxes from the paint store in the same building. We built display units with tea crates from Barbour's Teas. KENYA was stamped on their thin plywood sides— TANZANIA, NIGERIA. We covered them with burlap from the feed mill and made track lights out of apple juice cans, painted white. Another couple ran the store with us. Down the centre of the narrow store ran a low table, filled with white sand. Every morning, whoever's turn it was to work hand-picked dried flies from the sand, swirled fresh fingertip designs, made new arrangements: one teapot with four mugs; a tall vase filled with dried day-lily stalks. We kept our cash in a metal box, and a chair by the sales desk for visitors—often the old men who lived in the rooming house down the street.

I find myself doing two things at once, as we sit listening to the ringing tap of Jake's paintbrush on the edge of his water glass. I want to scoop up all my past selves—child, student, young mother, early middle-aged woman—and fold them into the person I am at this moment. I'm trying to see that all those me's are still here, while understanding, at the same time, that everything else—our store, the adding machine, the size of the spruce trees, radio programs—has gone or changed. Nothing will ever be the same, from one minute to the next. Yet moments flow, one into another. Reading philosophy when I was twenty, I encountered the notion that there can be no present moment, since time has either just passed or is just about to happen. In between loss and anticipation is—*what?* I glance at Peter. It's so unusual to see him this way, sitting with his sneakered feet flat on the floor, elbows on knees and hands hanging. *In between loss and anticipation is this,* I answer myself, whatever we may call it— momentum, rhythm, pulse. Yet if time flows like a river, there come moments when we realize that we've taken a fork, and the section we were travelling is far behind. Here we are, now: Jake on the studio porch, the sun sliding down into the southwest, baby swallows zigzagging over the garden. Suddenly, I feel that this is now, and that was then—as if we're no longer part of the same continuum; as if the past has formed, and I can see it, hanging like a cut flower, beginning to dry.

By late July the pastures are worn out. The horse and pony have spent their summer in the pasture that we see from our bedroom window. It rises on its west side in a steep bank overhanging the brook, spreads across the valley, runs along the edge of my vegetable garden, curves around to the back of the barn so the horse and pony, like the swallows, can go in and out whenever they wish. The animals fall into a pattern throughout high summer, spending from ten until four each day in the cool barn to escape the torment of fat flies that teem on their faces, udder-seeking deer flies, and blackflies that bloody the base of their ears. In late afternoon they emerge again and, as we eat supper on the porch, we see them browsing belly-deep in buttercups and clover, Minnie's tail flashing its henna highlights.

Cold nights diminish the insects. The soft-petalled wildflowers fade and are replaced by tougher flowers, with woody stems and dry leaves: purple steeplebush or the furzy Joe-Pye-weed. Thistles burst. Dusk carries chill air. When there's no grass left in the pastures, I string electric fencing around the mown hayfield and the marshy east pasture, where this year's marsh hawk hunts. The ground is dry and hard. Hoof prints are brittle and crumble at the edges. Brook trout circle in dwindling pools. Fence posts tip sideways, wires sag.

Predictably, our neighbour's cows escape. Their pasture, too, is depleted, and the young steers jump the fence. We wake to find them grazing on our front lawn or clopping down the driveway with heads held high. One morning Kevin opens the back door of their house and is startled to find a donkey staring in.

There's more space, everywhere. Thunderclouds thrust and pile, separating the seamless sky. Flowers grow in clumps. Herds drift, cows graze unclustered. Swallows fly so high they're like metal filings, glinting. Horses lift their muzzles and smell autumn on the air.

WHITE PEBBLES

On my birthday I wake early, before Peter. The bedroom door is open, and every room is filled with sleeping people: my parents, my brother and his wife, their two children, and Jake. I lie, remembering a line of Dylan Thomas: "It was my thirtieth year to heaven," and absorb the moment that will never come again—six o'clock on an August morning on the day when, for as long as I can remember, I have awaked feeling it's different from every other day in the year: the day of myself.

જી

AUGUST 10, 1995: *I want to stand and gaze at this place where I live—the great white clouds bundling up over the south hills, rising and evolving steadily and drifting eastwards; the weather-bleached barway white as bone. I don't want to be doing, making, digging, creating. I want to sit here and be. I feel so happy, lately. A steady, almost solitary happiness, a sense of wholeness and strength inside me. Recently, I realize that I can go into a room of people carrying my knowledge of myself like a secret and not care whether anyone sees it. I know it is there.*

A cool breeze whishes through the window-screen carrying the spicy scent of spruce needles, moss, river water. The breath of the wild intermingles with essence of farmhouse: cut grass, phlox, garden soil, porch shingles. The smell of northern summer is sharp, bracing; even the hottest day is held in this context of challenge.

I curl sleepily under the quilt, anticipating the peculiar ridiculousness of a family pulling on consciousness incrementally: one sock, then another; a dropped shoe; sleepy brushing of teeth; dazed staring over the rims of mugs. It is a rare event for this house to hold my entire nuclear family. When I was a child, no one lived far away from anyone else, and the gathering of family was commonplace, a simple Sunday routine. Women cooked, men carved, children giggled, we all washed dishes. Grown-ups in the front parlour afterwards. Children in the backyard in summer or, in winter, upstairs, playing with their fathers' toys in their ancestors' bedrooms. The cardboard lids of games boxes were soft, their edges burred, as were the pages of books and the cotton baubles of bedspreads. Things were repeated, regular as sunrise: a family grace, murmured in unison before dinner; lamb and mint jelly; jokes and pet names. As cars pulled out of the driveway, in late afternoon, Granny and Grampa would hurry from window to window, waving. I'd wave back easily, knowing they'd be there next week. I thought that family—like the untuned Steinway piano in my grandparents' dining room or the crystal bowls on their sideboard filled with Mello mints; like the round, hand-knit string face cloths and the smell of apples in the back hall—was something fixed, a house whose furniture never changed. Love was as abstract as death. Then, when I was ten years old, my grandfather died, and my child's world crumpled like a drawing over which I'd laboured and could never again smooth out.

My family is fragile as a flower garden, and the wild wind blows around us. I'll get out of bed and put on the coffee. I swing my feet over the edge of the bed and sit up.

"Happy birthday," Peter murmurs, reaching for me. And I swing my legs back up to curl sideways, put my arms around him.

❧

AUGUST 14, 1995: *Endless change. Things coming apart and knitting together again. Life is like a great creature breathing and sleeping and waking. Last summer I saw only dissolution. I was sickened by the red flame of a poppy on the morning it opened, seeing only the flower's demise. Now I release my desire for permanence, allow myself to sit on my heels in the warmth and feel the moment's splendour. I've yielded an element of my youth, lost a kind of passionate longing—gained patience.*

❧

The kids—Jake and his cousins Nate and Brinsley—want breakfast over fast. *Let's get there!* Where are the towels? We slap together sandwiches, seek Frisbee, binoculars, bird book, hats, sunscreen, beer. The screen door slams and slams.

Three cars tail one another. The road follows the contours of the land, leaving behind the geometry of farm valleys, climbing into rougher hills where the sky spreads like a desert over the grey slash and displaced boulders of clear-cut forests, snaking between the swelling mounds of blueberry barrens. Ravens soar with shining feathers. There are cabins and faded signs; then, like a slitted eye, the sea.

We pass through Fundy National Park. Perched on the clifftops are mown lawns, benches, and beds of zinnia, cleome, snapdragons. Windbreakers flutter as people unfold from parked cars clutching hats and leashed dogs; golfers stride with purpose. We drive through the village at the foot of the cliffs: smell of tar and creosote, of fried food and rotting seaweed. Mewing gulls hover over the boats at the wharf. I glimpse masts, ropes, the liquor store. Families with ice-cream cones ramble past gift shops, Ontario licence plates, a stuffed moose.

We cruise slowly through the village, ocean on one side, dark hills on the other. A river pours into sea-meadows, where great blue herons stand bent-necked, intent, one claw raised and curled. At a fish-and-chips shop, people sit at picnic tables sprinkling salt from paper packets. The silver-green grasses toss, and the river slides past banks of black mud.

We sweep through the town's sleepy morning and head east along the coast, pursuing my birthday desire: I want to be in a place where time is not managed, where events are without pre-conception. I want to launch my illusions, like a kite, into the sky and cut the string. As we turn off the main road, the threads that connect me to home fray and break. There are fewer and fewer houses. We pass abandoned farms with fields claimed by goldenrod and steeplebush. The road roughens. After miles of scraggly fir and spruce, the sky opens, the road winds over grassy bluffs. Fields spread around us, yet seem only a tiny part of the picture. Green grass, a white house, and a Canadian flag; far below, the ocean gracefully accepts the curve of land in tier on tier of foam-edged wave. My thoughts, like trapped birds, fly out into the sky and become small as the sandpipers, the gulls, and the black-backed ducks.

We park the cars and walk single-file down a narrow path. The teenagers run ahead; we adults follow, picking our way with care, hampered by all the gear we thought important so long ago this morning.

It's a wild beach, two miles of sand, tide wrack, and silvered driftwood. There's no one else here. We choose a tree carcass for our centre and put up a red and white striped beach umbrella. All our belongings lose coherence and become a jumble, instantly sandy. My father rolls up his pants and reveals his bony white feet. My mother tucks a piece of paper under the nose-piece of her glasses. They sit on bamboo mats under the umbrella. Sandpipers drop from the sky and stilt-walk in the surf, oblivious of my father's binoculars or the wind-rustled pages of my mother's tattered Gerald Durrell paperback.

Once we were a family of four: my brother and I, and my parents. We've multiplied, added two more families. Now my parents are back to being a unit of two. And, eventually, one of them will live alone. How solitary my son seemed when he came into the world, sprawled on the hostile air, fists clutching empti-ness as if he had lost an entire universe. How awed I was by his dignity. How I scrambled to fold him into the family batter, taught him to hold on tight.

I walk away from the umbrella until, when I look back, I can't tell if there are two specks under it or one.

We follow an impulse to separate, dispersing up and down the beach without discussion, aim, or plan; without guilt or negotiation. No one tries to organize the day. No one cares what time it is. The space and our smallness in it let us fly free.

Peter strides far down the beach, our little dog at his heels, until all I can see is the white spot of his canvas hat. Jake has made a beeline for the cliffs; he's splayed in a crevasse, seeking handholds. Brinsley drifts dreamily along the water's edge, sandals in one hand, dancer's legs loose at the hip, hair blowing across her face. Nate, twelve, is running, throwing, leaping, dodging, involved with sand, mud, sticks, wind. My brother and his wife have gone off alone, separately, like me and Peter; she's balancing on a log at the top of the beach, hand shielding eyes, squinting across the marsh at a solitary Baptist church. My brother stands with his arms folded across his chest, ball-cap shadowing his face, staring out to sea as though he's found something he's been looking for and will stand there all day.

Walking barefoot, studying the pebbles that mill and rattle in the surf's backwash, I want to dig my heels into this day and hold back the sun that slides up the sky so swiftly, once it has broken free of the lingering dawn. I can still be ruled by my heart because my mind tells me I should have learned, by now, not to regret the passing of time. This day, like all the days of summer, has been here before and will be here again. The sun, diamond pointed on the black, faceted waves, washing up over the red cliffs like morning light on flapping sheets. Gulls soaring sideways with dangling legs over pale, wind-combed grass. Sand crunchy with bleached crabs, twigs, dried seaweed. Salt wind, scoured driftwood. This wild bay on the Fundy coast, like the days of summer, will still be here in another thirty years.

I'm collecting white pebbles. The coloured ones lose their magic when they dry. I look for the ones that shine like eggs amid the mosaic of red-veined green, black-speckled red. I'm going to put these white pebbles in a white bowl, think of them as symbols for what endures.

I'm not warm enough, but I don't care, loving the freedom of baggy shorts and a flapping T-shirt. The ankle-deep water is icy, but I'm determined to be connected to all the pieces of this day: rock, tide, shadows, gull cry, crab scuttle, tide pool, cliff, sun, wind, sand, time, hunger, love. On my birthday I want to belong to this place.

A few miles up the coast, hundreds of thousands of sand-pipers are massed in a bay. They fly down from the Arctic every August and spend several weeks here, feasting on mud shrimp that teem on the surface as the tide retreats. The birds are build-ing their fat reserves, doubling their weight. They fly together in great thundering clouds to strengthen themselves. One day a cold front will move in, high tide will coincide with the end of the day, and the birds will orient themselves south-southeast and take wing, bound for the trade winds that will carry them to their wintering grounds in South America.

Three sandpipers have strayed from the flock. They run swiftly but don't seem to be pursuing anything. Their white underbellies shine as they skim the edge of the spent waves, claws skirting the frothy rope. Their feathers ruffle in the wind. They stop, peck rapidly, and then sprint ahead, long legs carrying their black and white bodies as effortlessly as the wings that, at any instant, might unfold and lift them into the sky.

I try to imagine myself inside a bird's body, try to imagine the sharp imperatives of a bird's life: *bubbles rising from sand, stop, peck; no falcon-shadow, keep running; spume, snail, sky.*

They've strayed, yes, but they know where their centre is. It's back around the cliffs, over a few bays on Mary's Point, where groups become flocks become mass. They're held to that centre. They'll sweep back to it, settle down like pebbles in a stream, toss and roil in the great, dark cloud of survival. Something startles them. Their wings stretch, they tiptoe on air, speed away close to the water, sure as arrows.

I look back, see my family. Under the vast unframed sea-sky we become our true size. We become the specks that we are and are absorbed. We are small the way the plovers, cutting northeast, are small. We are small the way the white pebbles are small. We are singular and not separate.

At the end of the open beach I think: *Odd how you can walk and walk on a beach and not feel that you've gotten anywhere. Nothing around you changes, you're kicking the frothing surf, the waves swell and peak and travel forward, relentlessly destroying themselves, and your legs assume the same rhythm. You keep going, with no destination, no goal. You walk in the light and the breath of the sea. You walk simply. Simply, you walk. And then you look back and are surprised to see that the place you started from has almost disappeared.*

I've carried myself a long way away from everyone else. Under the heat-trap of the red cliffs, the sand ends and I enter a world of rock. I scramble, leap, let the rocks direct my passage around tide pools, over slippery bladder seaweed. Waves meet rock cataclysmically, slither into crevasses, and spill out again. Jumping down, I find myself in my own hidden beach, a place where rocks rise all around. I sit on the warm sand, hugging my knees.

Everything moves. Sun, shadows, clouds, water, birds, the pebbles in the backwash. I lean back against smooth, sun-warm rock, and my hand travels sideways across it, idly, as though I'm stroking a horse's neck. Where is my centre? I roll the white pebbles in my palm. A cool breeze on my bare skin is tempered by heat, like ice cream in coffee. I think of the teenagers: Brinsley, dreaming at the edge of the sea in her sixteenth year; Jake, scaling cliffs, becoming the young man he imagined. I think of the long process of building oneself, the way these waves gather, tower, curl, and then spill from the mass when they reach the shore. I feel as if I'm back to the person who came into the world, back to the day of my birth, when, like my son, I came into the world reaching for life.

There's no sound but the pound and boom of waves. It's not a steady rhythm: there are pauses like long, indrawn breaths, anticipatory. In this pocket of rock and sand I'm scoured by sun, buffeted by wind. I wait for the next wave, feel the flick of gull-shadow on my face. One hand crunches sand, lets it spill. Rocks rise over my head. Sand gathers the heat. I'm alone on a wild coast, leaning against rock that has faced this water for a span of time against which I am a wisp of mist. And, gradually, the place involves me, overpowers me. The plangent cry of a gull, snatched by the wind. Barnacles, clustered in colonies. Seaweed, anchored on rocks, torn and wracked by the waves. The sea: cold, restless, merciless, endless, and without love.

I stand, pull myself back up the rock. There, in the distance, is the red and white striped umbrella. There, far away, is the white spire of the church steeple. People, wandering back towards beer and sandwiches.

Like the sandpipers I sprint with sudden speed back towards my family.

❧

Cross-legged, I succumb to the warmth of sweatshirt, jean jacket, and wool socks and pull a strand of hair from the corner of my mouth as I lean into my sandwich. Mum reads out loud about another family on another beach. The kids are scrabbling in the cookie tin, pretending to fight over it, tugging it back and forth until someone yells at them. Familiar irritations, family irritations, like a mosquito bite that you scratch without thinking. Sand in the pages of a paperback. Dad's beer tips over and he grabs it in a flash. Sand in beer on straw mat. Raspy seagrass. The dog trots happily towards us, soaking wet, saving her shake for our attention. A seagull struts, warily. We throw crusts. I'm child, parent, sister, wife. I'm me, jumping to my feet, running crazily past the teenagers, infected by their exuberance. They follow, and we run down the beach, dodging the water like soccer players. Heart racing, I reel towards Jake; he's ready for me, attacks, pretending to bite. Peter strolls down towards us—sunglasses, floppy hat. The rest of the family is tidying up from lunch, gathering binoculars, securing hats, preparing to join us.

The waves are smaller, subdued. The sun passes its apex and shines on the eastern cliffs. The wind strengthens. The gulls ride the wild sky. We veer down the beach, all of us, randomly, shouting, voices lost in the wind, blowing and anchored like an armada of kites, strings crossing.

❧

Late that afternoon we walk back up the trail, cross the field, get into our cars, and drive up the coast to Mary's Point. The light is low, rich. It doesn't glance and reflect the way it did when we set forth this morning but, rather, seeps into everything: the clapboards of houses, the petals of flowers. In the abandoned fields, pink fireweed smoulders.

We park by the dusty road and walk down a path through spruce trees. It's shadowed and cool under the trees, but on our left we glimpse a sunlit landscape, like another world—a salt marsh and the red mud banks of a tidal river; grasses that all sweep in the same direction, golden-green, textured by shadow.

We come out of the trees and step onto marram grass and sand. We're standing on a bank; below us is an estuary that empties into a wide bay. There are other people here, sitting on silvery logs, crouched over binoculars. Sandpipers cluster between the sand beach and the water. Their little round heads are like cobblestones. They run in spurts, as my three ran this morning; but here, dozens run simultaneously, setting off other dozens, until there's ripple on ripple of motion.

We walk quietly down to the beach and sit on a driftwood timber. I feel the fresh wind, the splintery wood under my legs. I smell mud, see the ragged spikes of dead trees, clumps of yarrow, banks of wild rose. I hear the thin splash of water, wind in the grasses, and the susurrant throat murmur of a quarter million birds.

I glance down the log. There's my entire family, elbows on knees, watching intently through binoculars like everyone else. Soon this summer visit will be over and everyone will leave, go separate ways. But right now, on this day of my birth, we're cobbled close, shoulder to shoulder, our unspoken love strong as light, and my pocket is filled with smooth white pebbles. I raise my own binoculars and spot a peregrine falcon. He spreads his wings and soars on the updraft over the cliffs.

ANOTHER FALL

THE WRITING CABIN

We've carried all of Jake's stuff upstairs, made a pile of boxes and suitcases in his bedroom. He's boarding with a young unmarried couple. They, too, are art students. There's a potter's wheel in a closet, two cats, and a back stairway to a dirt yard where they keep their bicycles locked to a porch railing. I notice unemptied ashtrays; herbs in pots on the kitchen windowsill; a smell of coriander and patchouli; a jumble of shoes at the top of the dark stairwell.

The couple are in the living room. I can hear them talking quietly and sense that they're dithering, not starting supper, since we said, no, we wouldn't stay, when invited. We should leave, but we linger in Jake's room. It's large, high-ceilinged, with a scarred wood floor. There's an overhead light, unshaded; a bed and a bureau. Its window overlooks an alley so narrow I can see the weave of the drawn curtains in the window just opposite. All the houses on this street seem slightly tipped, as if their foundations are off true. They're glazed with a residue of salty mist. Their paint—blue, green, red—is faded by North Atlantic gales.

Jake squats by a box, unfolds its flaps. He lifts something out with great care. It's a carving he worked on all summer. A bird, with runes. He sets it on the bureau.

Peter's pacing, peering out the window, testing the mattress

213

with his palms, opening and shutting a drawer. He's talking in a reasonable voice.

"Be *sure* to contribute. Not just pay your part of the bills, but help out. Don't leave your dishes sitting around. Keep an eye out for ways to help . . ."

"They seem like really nice people. Did you notice . . ." I draw his attention to things indicating homemaking: herbs, cookbook, cats.

I feel as if we're the seedlings that I sprout in spring and later have to separate. Their fibrous roots cling to one another, and I have to pull until they rip.

"We'll just go say goodbye to Jay and Susan," I offer. "Then we'll pop back in to say goodbye to you."

He sits back on one heel, looks at me and Peter. I glimpse the things in the box, last seen in his bedroom. What has he brought? A sheath knife; a carved wooden plate; books. I see them, and him, in the late afternoon light of a Halifax apartment.

He's looking at us as if we, too, are transfigured: smaller, perhaps, or older.

❧

It's ten o'clock when we arrive home. Peter turns off the engine and we sit for a minute before getting out. He reaches over and squeezes my hand. We listen to the ticking of the cooling engine. We're still with Jake in Halifax.

I step out. One cricket chirps, then another. The brook makes a solitary trickle. There's a dry rustling in the darkness: leaves, shivering.

Going into the house, our bodies make familiar motions. I tug the cord of the hall light. Peter reaches up to the key's hiding place. We shuffle our jackets onto hangers. The door makes its usual creak. Peter dumps mail on the table. I cross the dark room and flick the switch.

I go into the living room. We left a window cracked, and cool air breathes across the windowsill. The night is silent. Not a car passes on the valley road. The cows are no longer in their summer pasture across the driveway. I turn on the standing lamp and sit on the couch, in my winter corner. In the kitchen Peter makes small, preoccupied noises: the rip of an envelope, silence while he contemplates a bill, running water, a cupboard door opening.

Here it is, this moment that has been lodged in my imagination.

And I'm thinking about what to send over to Halifax: *fresh bread, a tin of homemade cookies, coffee beans, every few weeks. Does he have a grinder?*

Peter doesn't come to join me in the living room. I don't call to him. We respect the space between kitchen and living room. It's like the long miles between here and Halifax. I neither read nor pick up my knitting but float on the feeling of being on a threshold. It's the place that my philosophy teacher told me didn't exist: somewhere in between. I wonder when I'll step over the edge and begin the next epoch. Perhaps when Peter and I go upstairs to bed, or when we wake up tomorrow morning in the childless house.

It's a place of calm. I find myself thinking about my hands, as if all my feelings are centred there. The shape of a baby's head; a flannel pillowcase, stretched taut; zippers; soapy face cloths.

My hands are relaxed, cupped. I'm surprised to feel the house becoming quiet rather than silent. Ash trickles in the flue. Leaves sigh. Light touches the heather-blue skeins of yarn in my knitting basket. It's neither an ending, this moment, nor a beginning. Within it I sense the person I'm still becoming.

๑ๅ

Jake's been in Halifax for a week. We've talked to him on the phone twice. He's pleasant, but he resists our perceptions and has no intention of taking us with him into his new life.

Peter is reorganizing the studio, moving wheels and ware boards, building new work surfaces and kilns, beginning the end of his days as a production potter and heading towards riskier territory. I've been turning out closets, taking clothes and shoes to the Salvation Army, digging into the back of the pantry, rooting in cupboards. We've both been utterly preoccupied, precipitating chaos. Just now the kitchen is covered with bags of ancient dried beans, boxes of pancake mix, empty food colouring jars, hard marshmallows and dusty cocoa powder, antiquated homemade dill beans.

I go onto the back porch. It's been raining for days and, in the pasture, my black horse shines like a seal; spiderwebs sag. The air smells of sodden leaves, and the hills are scarfed by mists that shift imperceptibly, softening colours, blending dark spruce with red maple, diffusing yellow poplar, making the forests hushed, like a foggy sea.

I decide to go for a walk, and I stop in at the studio on my way to the woods. "Come for a walk?" but Peter is stirring plaster, breathing like Darth Vader through a respirator. He shakes his head and waves me on.

Every blade of grass is bent by water droplets. A bird calls, one sweet note, and then there's the cry of a blue jay, a double-edged sound, like biting into a sour plum. The wild raspberry leaves are riddled with holes, whitened around the edges. Like healed wounds, I think, holding one in my hand. In the hedgerow are the wind-tattered remnants of summer: the drenched fluff of golden-rod, brown spires of steeplebush. The old orchard, six gnarled trees, crouches in the hollow between woods and hill. There's a peculiar swirl in the grass, and I kneel to investigate, soaking the knees of my jeans. It's a ground nest, sculpted of blades of living grass, bent double, woven into a round hanging cup. The nest is lined with matted fur, now sodden. Sitting back on my heels, I imagine the featherlight eggs that hung there. Soon it will vanish, this marvellous creation.

I scramble over a rockpile and follow our footpath that curves around beds of wild blueberries, red-leaved. The path crosses a high meadow and enters the woods. Spruce boughs hang low, heavy with raindrops. My feet make no sound on the cushiony path that passes collapsed hay-scented ferns, rises up the hillside, and then switchbacks down to the brook, ending at a pool. It's full of water again, as it was in June, when blue-flag iris grew at its edge. A small waterfall spills into it. I sit on a log, watching slabs of rock through the clear water; where the current rills, the rock seems soft, wavering, as if it, too, is fluid.

There's a rush, a pattering. It begins to rain, and the black water is creased by silver bullets. Close by, the rain has individual voices: a splat on a bunchberry leaf, a tap on a mossy rock.

Up on the hillsides, the rain strokes the forest with a muted, watery rustle.

I pull up my hood. Across from me, maples and birches rise up the steep hill until they step into the veil of mist and vanish. Their trunks are rain-darkened. Yellow leaves detach from the weight of water. One by one they fall, and the trees lose the mantle that whirled around them, shivering, light-struck, roaring, sighing. The leaves waver, wander down the air, come to a rest.

I'm calm. It surprises me, like the quiet of the house on the night of our return from Halifax. Things are as they should be. Jake's departure is a solid fact now, as real as the nest beneath the apple tree. Time passes, time approaches. Here, on the edge of both, is peace.

❦

One morning, in the last week of September, I go out to the barn and get the wheelbarrow. I park it at the back door of the house. The swallows are long gone. Even the spiderwebs are frayed; broken silk trails from the weathered door frame, and I wonder where they winter, those fat grey spiders.

It stormed all night. The wind was from the northeast, so we slept with our window tight shut, listening to the drumming pummel of rain, like blunt fingertips. This morning the air is astringent, having lost its sleepy moisture, and it slaps me with the promise of winter. I pass our cross-country skis hanging on the woodshed wall, walk through the kitchen, and continue up the stairs. I'm moving my office to the sauna bath, which is completely renovated. I'll work there until its Little Cod wood stove can no longer keep me warm.

I load up the wheelbarrow with things I'll need in my writing cabin, then push it up over the pasture. The horse and pony prick their ears, stand stock-still watching me until I vanish into the trees.

At the sauna bath I walk up the outside staircase, running my hand along the peeled tamarack railing, push open the door into the steep-ceilinged little room, and open all the windows. The east window looks onto a grove of spruce trees, so close that, when I sit at my desk, I see nothing but heavy branches stirring languorously. The door and a small-paned window open onto the second-floor deck and overlook the clearing where we made our bonfires last winter. Asters, thistles, and goldenrod have replaced the beds of forget-me-nots and buttercups. On the ridge, the last coppery poplar leaves flutter against a blue sky.

Before going back down for the contents of the wheelbarrow, I sit at my writing table with my journal, absorbing the simplicity of the place. The floor is cheap-grade spruce, knotty, painted green. The wood stove is designed for a boat's cabin, its squat iron legs slotted for screws. Stacked along the wall behind it are miniature stove-wood logs, split fine, one-foot long. Against another wall is a blue bookcase with a kerosene lantern on its top shelf. A painting Jake made when he was four years old hangs there: a red house like a wizard's tower in a snowy field, beneath a star-studded sky. A rocking chair sits next to the stove, and behind it on a beam is a tin of matches and two pottery mugs. Wooden pegs hold a fly swatter, a dustpan, and a whisk broom. A blue-handled broom leans against the spruce wall.

❧

SEPTEMBER 25, 1995: *Strangely, it takes courage to sit at this table and begin to write in my journal. This morning I walked away from the house feeling as though I were forgetting something. Perhaps it was all the distractions that have become so familiar. Now I'm trying on my longing, like a beautiful dress that I raise my arms for and let slip over my head, fearing it will not, after all, fit or be becoming.*

❧

I take up the broom and begin sweeping the floor. In a corner next to the door I sweep and sweep in the same place and still more emerges—desiccated insect parts, spruce needles, dead lady bugs—coming as if from some endless source, like sand through a crack. I sweep the pile into the dustpan and take it onto the deck, begin to toss it into the wind, but pause and carry it to my writing table instead. I stir through the pile with the point of a pencil. It's a hoard, I realize, perhaps the collection of a lifetime. Nothing is bigger than a mouse paw. There's a ladybug's carapace, shiny as old shellac, seven black dots grouped around a triangle. I move my pencil through the dustpan, wondering how a mouse might carry a ladybug. A minute piece of dried flower, blue, with pleated corners, its stamen still yellow. The fragment retains a wistful presence, and I think of my own hoard, the flowers I've pressed in the pages of books, the locks of hair I've found in old Bibles. I find flies' wings; wasps' wings, longer, sleeker, tinged with iridescence. Spruce needles and mouse droppings, pieces of dried grass and a moth's wing, dark brown with four white spots. A boat-shaped seed, smaller than a radish seed, hard as a pebble, with an oval hole chewed or drilled. Another seed, with a similar hole. Dried bud-tips from fir trees, the dust that gathers behind boards, and a piece of lichen, like a snow-flattened mitten. I pick up a scrap of hairy, tarred string: oakum. *A chandler's shop, thirty years ago. Gasoline sheening the harbour's water, and seagulls spread-winged, dropping past its red shingles. We carried the barrel-shaped bales of oakum—tar on our sleeves—and brought them up here to the woods. We laid strips between the logs as we built the first sauna bath.* A wood chip. *Peter's axe; he's twenty-four years old, swings at the waist supple as a sapling, flattening one side of a log.* Something crisp and white. A piece of paper the size of a pea, with a folded corner. *Like the paper hats we made for Jake when he was a baby.* A pebble. *Might have been imbedded in my hiking boot after walking at the bay.*

I lean closer, put down my pencil. I hook my finger under something that appears to be pale blue string. I lift it. It droops over my finger like a necklace. Sun lies across the table, and I move the thread into its path. The thread is suspended within a tube of dust in which are embedded yellow bees' legs, slivers of kindling, mica, wings, broom straw, a strand of my own hair. The dust necklace hangs from my finger, beautiful, bizarre—like a necklace at an exhibition of contemporary jewellery. I let it fall back onto the formless heap in the dustpan.

Someday, someone will go through my stuff. I imagine a grand-daughter. Years after Jake dies, she inherits the house. She goes into my office, which has been left untouched for fifty years. *Who carved,* she'll think, *this walking stick, decorated with* runes? Was it Dad? She won't know that they're finding-spells, or that he was seventeen when he made it. She'll find a faded, hand-drawn card. *Happy Birthday*, it says, every letter a body part. The *B* is two buttocks wearing a belt. *That must have made her laugh!* she'll think. *Oh look! Two silver bracelets, hand made. And a turquoise ring.* She opens a wooden box. Inside are white pebbles, a snipe skull, and a railroad spike shedding rust. In a drawer are postcards fastened with a disintegrating rubber band. A carved wooden angel. Another box, cedar, containing a shilling, a half-penny, and a half-crown. A pressed yellow rose with a clipping of a beautiful blonde princess holding an African child. A turtle shell. A stuffed dog with no eyes.

And she remembers me, I think. I'm there in that room. I'm in the wind that she feels on her face, I'm in the earth she digs, the wildflowers she picks. Just as I'm in this dustpan. Remnants of me, gathered by a mouse. One day I'll lie under the sky; I'll bleach, dissolve, run into the river, wash into iris roots.

I carry the dustpan to the deck and shake the contents windwards. The mouse has outlived its time. It doesn't watch as I send its hoard drifting.

I go down the stairs and begin gathering my office from the wheelbarrow. Dictionary, pencils, reams of paper. I can feel it in my heart, like pressure—what I'm going to write.

THE SAUNA BATH

It's mid-October. The garden is empty, save for dried stalks and weeds. The potato patch is like a furrowed field, the soil tossed into ridges. Once again, blue jays have scoured the 'Mammoth Russian' sunflower heads, and now their seed pods are as empty as the wasps' nests, the spiderwebs.

The harvest is squirrelled away. Crates of potatoes are stacked in the root cellar. Winter squash cover the woodshed floor; in the laundry room, string bags of garlic and onions are suspended from nails. It's the same as every October since we began living in this house. Chard, green beans, and broccoli in the freezer. Bunches of sage and summer savoury hanging from the wooden pegs behind the stove. Firewood in the cellar. Storm windows in place, windows caulked on the inside. Our winter coats shifted from the end of the coat rack to the beginning. Wool socks, gloves. The smell of frost and a quiet sky.

This year, though, we've begun to have a sauna bath most Saturdays.

Peter spends the afternoon walking up through the pasture. I can see smoke rising from the trees, a renewed plume with every one of his visits. I make soup, using our own garden's onions, garlic, carrots, potatoes. Sage crumbles in my palm, its grey-green flakes drift on the steaming water. The kitchen smells of herbs and cornbread. The sun sets at six, and we eat. We talk about our projects. Peter's experimenting with glass and bronze, sending slides to galleries. I've conceived a new project and have started writing; the editor is several steps closer to convincing her publisher that my book should be published. We remind ourselves of how, at this time of year, we're usually preparing for the Toronto show: getting out the display; ordering gift boxes, tissue paper, and sales books; filling shelves with vases, bowls, and teapots; sending out invitations; preparing for a weekend show in our own studio before we go to Toronto; glazing, firing, packing. Now we're in free fall, our income uncertain, living off our savings, wondering if the parachute is going to open.

After supper, Peter goes up to stoke the fire one last time. When he returns, he reports that the temperature of the sauna is 200 degrees Fahrenheit. We do the dishes, change the sheets on our bed, fill backpacks with towels, bathrobes, bottles of water, and a Thermos of tea. We leave the house at dusk, when the first stars have pricked the sky. We walk up over the pasture, carrying a kerosene lantern whose light swings in a narrow bar, finding dead goldenrod and dried grasses.

When we arrive at the sauna, I take Peter's backpack and climb the stairs. I push into the little room, set down the packs, and light candles. Then I go back onto the deck and lean on the railing to watch as Peter empties the firebox, leaving only the hot rocks to maintain the sauna's temperature. He fills a snow shovel with red embers. They streak the dark as he tosses them into a pile, where they pulse like slitted dragon's eyes. He comes up the stairs when everything is ready: a trash can of water that's been heating on the stove; buckets of icy river water on the slatted wood floor; the loofah sponges where we can reach them. Here, upstairs, the room is cozy, warmed by the hot sauna just beneath, the resinous hot-log scent seeping through the floorboards. Shadows tip and fall in the candlelight as we undress. Going back down the stairs, naked beneath my terry-cloth robe, my hand rides the twists of the smooth tamarack railing, and I hear the thin trickle of the brook. Smoke wisps from the coal pile, tinges the air.

We sit, naked, on the top bench. In the dim light of a battery-powered bulb, the logs are the colour of our skin. Concealed beneath an iron hood, beach stones are presences, radiating heat. There's nothing to do but sit, sweat, or lie down. I roll up my towel, put it behind my head, stretch out. My heart speeds as sweat prickles my scalp, a bead rolls down my face. We don't talk. We're waiting without pressure. At some point the heat will be unendurable. Then the black water waits, under starlight.

Everything waits and moves. Our hearts, beating. The stars, wheeling over the spruce trees. The dip pool: deep, round, its surface unrippled, river fed.

We are quiet and the night's life rises around us—sigh of branch, tick of cooling rock.

Here, everything has its place: a ladle hangs from a wooden peg; our towels and robes, shadowed; wooden bucket, with face cloth and warm water, close at hand. We'll follow this ritual of bathing as need dictates. I go out first, less able to endure the heat. Peter follows, and we pick our way down over a path through thistles and goldenrod. *Don't think.* Ice water; already I'm gasping, flailing for Peter's hand. He hauls me out onto the bank. The caul of heat is gone, sweat is washed away, I hear Peter's whoop as he plunges. His skin begins to steam as soon as he scrambles out of the water.

Down across the meadow we can see a square of light: our bedroom window. And the angle of our farmhouse roof, darker than the sky. The night air no longer feels cold but is balmy, caressing my skin. I feel a pleasant dizziness as I tip my head back. We stand, naked and steaming, watching the stars. There's Cassiopeia, the Pleiades. And there, just over the barn, is the Big Dipper. I tuck my hands into my armpits. Peter's pointing to another constellation that he thinks he knows. How many years, I wonder, did we live on this farm—building, making, striving—before we began to learn the stars?

The pile of coals flares, subsides. It makes tiny tickings, alive in the darkness like the brook or the sighing spruce branches.

We stand for a long time, until our feet begin to cool. Then the hot, spruce-scented sauna beckons. We walk back, stepping carefully along a board that spans the brook. The little cabin sits on its knoll, the kerosene lamp hanging from a beam, candlelight glowing from the upstairs window.

I glance up as we step under the trees. There's Orion, climbing the sky.

ACKNOWLEDGMENTS

Thanks to Craig Pyette, Kelly Hill, Scott Sellers, Sheila Kay, Deirdre Molina, Allyson Latta, and, especially, Rosemary Shipton.

Special thanks, for enthusiasm, guidance, and trust, to Angelika Glover and Diane Martin.

Thanks, always, to my terrific agent and friend, Jackie Kaiser.

Thanks to Pat, Kevin, Dan, Chris, Nick, and Zane McCaig; Sue McKay; Pete, Jude, and Maya Williams; Mark Davis; Wendell and Alison Davis; Mary Wilkins; Marilynn Mair; Amy Carpenter-Tonning and Alyson Scott; Mark Connell; Bob and Kathy Osborne; Dr. S. Khedheri; Andy Powning; Marjorie Pagett; Brinsley and Nathaniel Davis: all of whom appear in this book.

Thanks to Sara, Maeve, and Bridget, for keeping me cheerful. Thanks to my son, Jake, whose ideas nourish me. And thanks, most of all, to my husband, Peter, attentive reader and beloved woods-walking companion.

PERMISSIONS AND CREDITS

Grateful acknowledgment is made to the following for permissions to reprint quotations included in this book:

Quote from *The Hero with a Thousand Faces*, by Joseph Campbell, Abacus Edition, printed in Great Britain 1975 by Sphere Books Ltd., copyright 1949 by Bollingen Foundation Inc., New York, p. 30.

Lines from "Pine Tree Tops" and "The Bath," by Gary Snyder, from *Turtle Island*, copyright 1974 by Gary Snyder. Reprinted by permission of New Directions Publishing Corp.

Line from "Poem in October," by Dylan Thomas, from *The Poems of Dylan Thomas*, copyright 1945 by the Trustees for the Copyrights of Dylan Thomas, first published in Poetry. Reprinted by permission of New Directions Publishing Corp.

"Who Has Seen the Wind?" by Christina Rossetti, from *Sing-Song, A Nursery Rhyme Book*, George Routledge and Sons, London, 1872.

Lines from "I Think Continuously of Those Who Were Great," by Stephen Spender, *New Collected Poems*, ed. Michael Brett, Faber and Faber, 2004.

Quote from Robert Frost, from *Selected Prose of Robert Frost*, ed. Hyde Cox and Edward Connery Lathem, copyright 1939, copyright 1967, Henry Holt and Co., Inc.

Quote from John Muir from "Windstorm in the Forests," in *The Mountains of California*, originally published by Appleton-Century-Crofts Inc., as excerpted in Green Treasury, by Edwin Way Teale, Dodd, Mead and Co., New York, 1952, pp. 183, 184.

BETH POWNING is the author of *Seeds of Another Summer: Finding the Spirit of Home in Nature*, *Shadow Child: An Apprenticeship in Love and Loss*, and, most recently, the novel *The Hatbox Letters*. She lives in Sussex, New Brunswick, with her partner, the artist Peter Powning.